THE HEART BREAK HOTEL

HOW LONG WILL YOU STAY?

JOEY FURJANIC

CROSSBOOKS
PUBLISHING

CrossBooks™
A Division of LifeWay
1663 Liberty Drive
Bloomington, IN 47403
www.crossbooks.com
Phone: 1-866-879-0502

First published by CrossBooks 2/24/2012

ISBN: 978-1-4627-1274-8 (sc)
ISBN: 978-1-4627-1275-5 (e)

Library of Congress Control Number: 2012931042

Printed in the United States of America

This book is printed on acid-free paper.

Dedication

I dedicate this book to my parents, Pat and Joe Furjanic. Without a doubt, you are truly my best friends and heroes. There is no one else I look toward quite like you. Thank you for listening, thank you for daring to try anything and always instilling confidence within me. It does not make sense that I have been able to go where I've gone, do what I've done, and live how I live. Any accomplishments, any souls, any victories, we share in this eternal crown. All praise and glory to heaven for you. And as we always say, if I don't see you here, see you on the other side. I love you.

Additionally, I dedicate this book to the students and leaders who changed my life from 2008 to 2010. That city and this world are still yours for the taking. Your promise is my constant hope. I love you for the rest of my life and I am always yours.

Acknowledgments

I want to thank and acknowledge a few people who have invested their time and resources into my life. This is just a small thank you to those who have provided me some great opportunities.

Thank you Mainstream Orlando and Faith Assembly in Orlando. I know what I know and I am who I am because of your great influence. There are so many of you who have played a role in my development throughout the years, and it brings great joy to my soul to reminisce on this incredibly important phase of my life. Thank you again.

Thank you to the Oaks Fellowship in Dallas. I am forever grateful that you gave a young guy like me a shot. This book derives partly from our time together.

Thank you to my family in Mesquite as well as New Community Church. You hold my blood, tears, sweat, and joy. You are forever in my heart.

Thank you to GT Christian Life in New York and the iMatter Foundation. You have taken care of me like I was one of your own. You epitomize the Gospel in your generosity and compassion.

Thank you, Roger Coles, for always taking care of my graphic and website needs. You are always available for me, and more than anything, I am so glad we are friends. Not only do you do quality work, you are a quality minister. Thanks for doing the artwork for this project. Blessings to you!

Thank you, Manwell Reyes, for flying into Dallas all those times and lending your creative juices to my team. You didn't have to do that and you always did it for nothing in return. You helped us formulate this idea and lives were changed because of it.

Thank you, Sean Anderson and Shayna DuPre', for taking a look at this project and helping me make some sense of it. You guys are brilliant! Also, Bart Willoughby, thank you for correcting all my theological mishaps. You are a brother, friend, and confidant. Donnie Petty, there are not enough words that could describe our covenant; we are for life. Thank you for your friendship and commitment.

Thank you, Tim Ross, for writing the foreword to this book. I call you pastor, teacher, and mentor. I am eternally grateful for your willingness to invest in me.

Thank you, Lauren Lowmaster, for working countless hours on this project. There is no way this could have ever gotten done without you. Thank you for teaching me how to serve, love, and give. What God has done in you has changed me forever.

Content Summaries

Part 1 – Checking In

Chapter 1: **First Time in a Hotel**   1

Whether young or old, each and every individual has experienced heartbreak and disappointment at some point in his life. This chapter introduces the concept of pain and disappointment from the very first experience. We go deep immediately, looking back at our pasts to identify what may have brought us into this hotel in the first place.

Chapter 2: **Exploring the Hotel**
(The Choice Chapter/Four Levels of Burn)   19

Once we settle into the room (our initial pain), we generally like to explore the hotel. This is where we get comfortable with our surroundings. Because we are exploring this new venue, our initial pain goes into hiding and we begin to cope with life on the inside. At this level, we can pinpoint the beginning of our pain more clearly. Sadly, some destructive behavior becomes okay; exploration to cover up hurt still feels awkward but somewhat necessary. This chapter is ultimately about making the difficult, but right choices and how we can practically implement them into our daily lives.

Probably the most fun part about being in a hotel room is jumping on a bed that isn't yours. This feels carefree—no rules and no consequences. Well, until something breaks, of course. We tend to be so comfortable and carefree about the mess and the pain that we are in that we lose all sense of responsibility, passion, conviction, and discernment. Things begin to break; we get more in debt to sin and pain. But sooner or later, jumping on the bed gets boring and we are left leaning over the balcony.

Part 2 – Room Service

Chapter 4: **Bill My Room
(Danger Zone)** 48

Most of us have been guilty of searching for love rather than letting love find us. Whether that is in romantic relationships or friendships, we tend to be searchers rather than patient waiters. This chapter deals with the danger of lust and the concept of love our culture has created. This is such a danger zone because we set ourselves up for disappointment and loneliness when our expectations for people don't match what Playboy, MTV, or mainstream media portrays. This racks up our bill in the hotel, making it more and more difficult to ever get out.

Chapter 5: **Stuck in the Room** 70

This chapter is really part two of our focus on lust. Our discussions will be based in less of a sexual context and directed more towards the lust for more: having more, wanting more, needing more, etc. This concept keeps us stuck in the hotel—we miss out on the beauty of life by trying to secure the most from life. We burn bridges and hurt people by lusting for more. We find that it is healthy to dream and be driven to succeed, but there is also a contrast to those dreams that can bind us. Being stuck in the room shows us the difference between having urgency about getting out of our awful, sometimes self-induced circumstances and being content with the gifts and blessings we have been given in life. We will learn that it is possible to be urgent and content, passionate and peaceful.

Part 3 – Housekeeping

Chapter 6: **The Mirror Test**   **82**

Full of exercises in confession and honesty, we will begin to build accountability within our current relationships. In addition, this is a call for help to our friends and families. Housekeeping means that it is time to clean up! This might be one of the most uncomfortable chapters as we take a look into the mirror and look at what we have become. Can we even recognize who we used to be, or worse, what we could have been? Let's clean up this regret and become powerful again—or for the first time!

Chapter 7: **Do Not Disturb**
(The Relationship Chapter)   **94**

All of us have an internal threshold of boundaries we aren't ever willing to cross, would maybe cross, and would easily cross if presented. We have to take the "Do Not Disturb" sign off our door and begin cleaning up. The only way we can do that is to define the areas in which we are willing to compromise our integrity and character. We walked into the hotel with suitcases full of a dirty wardrobe of heartbreak; now we have to decide what we are willing to wash and what we are willing to keep dirty and hidden. Parameters of right and wrong, good and bad, helpful and helpless will be defined clearly here.

Part 4 – Checking Out

Chapter 8: **Packing Your Bags
(The Forgiveness Chapter)**   113

Once we begin to pack up our old stuff, we realize how nasty it is. We see how discolored and out of style our old clothes really are. We know we have to get out of this hotel but have no ride home, and there is so much baggage that we can't bear the thought of carrying it all downstairs. So what is the solution? Leave it all here! Leave it all behind! Once the decision has been made, we find that forgiveness is the key that unlocks the door to freedom.

Chapter 9: **Pay the Bill**   132

With the amount of time we have stayed in the hotel and the extra services we've tapped into, we will never be able to pay the steep bill we accrued. The concierge and manager of the hotel begin to pressure us to stay longer. They say we will be able to pay for it at another time in life. Thankfully, we realize the necessity of getting out and getting out now. Unfortunately, we just don't know how. Thankfully, Jesus already paid the bill and called you a taxi! The cost is that we have to go with him, and his road isn't always easy or luxurious. But it is full of freedom and redemption which we desperately need. Go! Let generosity and compassion be the currency of restoration. We cannot let anyone convince us otherwise!

Chapter 10: **Going Shopping (The Holy Spirit Chapter)** 147

The last thing we must do is go shopping because the clothes we left at the hotel represent our old self, not our brand-new opportunity. It is time to put on a new garment of hope, prosperity, and promise. We are headed straight for a new life, with new people, new values, and a real savior.

Foreword

I travel. *A lot.* As a relational evangelist, I have traveled to nearly every state in America and have been halfway around the world. I have stayed in some of the nicest hotels you could ever imagine, and I have stayed in hotels that left a permanent stain upon my psyche. Soiled sheets. Cold showers. No air-conditioning. Bad food. No food. You name it, and I have probably had at least one experience with it during my many years of travel ...

It is hard to travel to as many places, as many times as I have and not run into a bad hotel. It's inevitable that you will find yourself in a place where you ask yourself, "What am I doing here?" Sometimes it's someone else's fault, other times it's our own; nevertheless, the question must be answered ...

At times, life has a way of taking us on a journey that we didn't necessarily book a ticket for and dropping us off at a place of disappointment, discouragement, hopelessness, and heartbreak. Honestly, I can tell you I have been in every single one of these hotels, but by far, the Heartbreak Hotel has been the worst.

This hotel is an empty place. There are no pictures on the walls, no host to greet you, nor is there any room service you would want to order. Everyone is bitter, angry, and heartbroken.

The saddest part of all: *this place never has any vacancy*. There is a line outside the door. And while I don't think people set out to stay there, once inside, some stay years too long—others stay their entire lives.

Please understand—this hotel isn't found in one place, one race, or even one specific side of town. Heartbreak Hotel is a chain. A chain of bondage that only the power of the Holy Spirit can run out of business.

We were not meant to live heartbroken lives. We were not meant to accept heartbreak as normalcy. We were created to live our lives with hearts that beat with joy and freedom! I am thrilled that Joey has decided to write this book, and I believe that every chapter will help to identify a place in your life where you have stayed in a room at this Heartbreak Hotel.

Know that this book is written from experience, and its truths will bring freedom to all who hear it. It's time to check out of the Heartbreak Hotel. Leave your things, and throw away the room key. Your Father is calling, and it's time to come home!

Tim Ross
Tim Ross Ministries
www.timross.org

Introduction

Hotel Construction

Not long ago, I was a youth pastor in a rowdy, urban town east of Dallas. Some like to think of that town as the place where the rodeo became famous, but I like to think of it as the town where hope became contagious. It is quite funny; when I arrived, there was barely a building for the church and there weren't any students at all inside that tiny place. What happened next changed my thoughts, my ideals, and everything I used to think was important. Beyond that, what took place was an infusion of direction for lives that seemed to drift without any rhyme or reason.

Our group started with zero students, little money, and without even a room in which to meet. I met this quirky, fourteen-year-old Puerto Rican girl whose father loaned me a map of Dallas. My initial thought, *how in the world could I build a group with this fourteen-year-old student?* What was I going to do, take her to lunch? Immediately, I asked her if she knew any boys. Like most teenage girls, she knew many. Of those, only two were willing to come. On the bright side, we grew from zero to four in minutes (I counted myself!)! From what I could tell, these two hyper-active boys really liked this young lady, so I figured I would use that to my advantage: wherever she would go, they would follow. We started to hang out anywhere and everywhere we could find a space. It seemed like each week, more and more of these crazy kids would follow us around—maybe because I spent my short life's savings on ice cream, but who knows? Sure enough, there were more than a hundred of them within a matter of months, and many more followed in the next months and year. Needless to say, I had to stop buying ice cream all the time.

Here I was, a twenty-two-year-old young man, in over my head and loaded with responsibility. The fear of letting these kids down gripped me intensely. Their well-being and success became my reason for waking up in the morning. And getting to know them had quickly become my greatest joy. Up to this point, I had never met students, or people for that matter, who were so open and honest. We experienced a plethora of tears, love, and accomplishment. It was so *me*, right up my alley. Even though they were open and honest, these were also some of the most cynical, neglected young people our great land could produce. I called them "Mess," short for our town, Mesquite. In a weird way, they loved it; they craved a little bit of name-calling (only from me, of course).

As our group grew, I needed to be conscious of continuing to create a culture of family. When it first began, it was small, easy to stay focused and honest. The more people came, the more intentional I had to be about the depth of our content and making sure we were really discussing things that mattered. How was I going to do that? What theme could we, as a group, live by, lean on together, struggle with together, and be victorious through together? Finally it came to me ...

At some point in *everyone's* life, he has experienced disappointment or heartache; and if he hasn't, he will. I had to capitalize on my newfound revelation; I knew this was where we were going to come together for life. This is how the Heartbreak Hotel was birthed. We created a three-week teaching series full of acting, music, dancing, and a Gospel presentation. So many people came! From parents to students (including middle school through college), it was the start of something contagious: *hope*. But it wasn't just a three-week message series; it became the message of everything we did. If you were full of pain and despair, brokenness and heartache, we were the vehicle that took you to hope and happiness, peace and freedom.

For all who checked into this hotel of heartbreak, there was a way to check out. Somebody had paid the bill. From every visitor to every regular, everyone knew this: *check out and stay out!* But if you checked back in, we were always there to help you get out again. Furthermore, we were fully committed to each other. We committed to watching the backs of our family. If someone was new, we would help him find his way. If someone was struggling, we would be there. Literally, no man was left behind; no one was going to get left inside the hotel! There you have it, the concept of the Heartbreak Hotel.

To me, there is nothing quite like watching life be injected into the veins of people of any age—kids, students, and adults, even an entire city. Throughout this book, I want to share with you how hope can overwhelm a life that has been suffocated by heartbreak and disappointment. You are going to hear funny stories, ridiculous stories, and heartbreaking stories, but above all, you will have an opportunity to check out of your own hotel of heartbreak. You will be able to put on a new outfit of life, hope, and direction. Your family situation can be different, and some of you will actually see light guiding your once-dark future. If you so choose, you're going to finally leave behind that suitcase of despair. Now is the time. Won't you join me?

(PART 1 – CHECKING IN)

CHAPTER 1: **FIRST TIME IN A HOTEL**

You can clutch the past so tightly to your chest that it leaves your arms too full to embrace the present. -Jan Glidewell

<u>Nice to Finally Meet You</u>

I once met a man who taught me everything I ever needed to know about love. Not only did he share everything I needed to know, he wrote it down for me to share with you. In fact, this book you are about to read is simply a reflection of and a response to my conversation and experience with this man's story.

My name is Joey, and for however long it takes you to read this book, I will be your teammate and partner in this hotel check out process. That's right, hotel check out! Everyone, child to student, adult to senior, will check into the hotel of heartbreak at some point; it is just the nature of this world. But everyone has the opportunity to check out of this mess as well. I am simply here to help you do that.

Let me commend you; somehow or another you were daring and gutsy enough to open up this book. Please believe that you are about to take a journey right into the core of your soul. To get there, we have to navigate our way through some dark hallways, filthy rooms, and molded ceilings. Oh, and if you haven't noticed by now, we are in an old hotel, the Heartbreak Hotel that is. This prison-like hotel has facilitated death row since the beginning of time. Even still, our intrepid journey will bring great joy, arouse deep pain, but most important, it will be the catalyst for freedom unlike anything we have ever known. No man needs to be left behind; we have the distinct opportunity to sooth our souls and evacuate this hotel, together.

This book is simply about our lives and the reality that hurt and disappointment linger on this earth. In this life, we will never be exempt from the disease of pain, but we most certainly can live with peace and freedom through anything that might come our way. You, like me, have a daily opportunity—a choice, if you will.

Like I said, at some point, we have all checked in to this dangerous hotel of heartbreak, but are we willing to check out and *stay* out? That is the ultimate question, the driving theme behind why this book exists. I am here to exclaim to you that I survived the Heartbreak Hotel! I have checked out, *but* my survival is based on a daily decision to stay out. This is the hard part; the main part I am going to teach you.

Are you ready yet? To be honest, I was not even ready to write it. The hotel process brings forth the darkest secrets and the deepest insecurities. Somehow, though, I got through it. Guess what—you will too! You will be better for it, more powerful from it, and the strongest *you* you've ever been. This book will help catapult you toward your destiny, your life's purpose.

Now, before we dig into this book, I have to confess something: only recently have I begun to understand the concept of true love. See, the man I spoke of earlier was deeply in love. His was the kind of in-love that everybody hates. You know the type—where the couple makes everyone sick by how they act in public with each other. This was the couple that could not keep their hands, eyes, or emotions hidden. They could barely *breathe* without the other person. It almost felt like they had enough chemistry to set off a bomb resulting in World War III!

Really, you could tell that they made everyone else jealous of what they had. To men, it was inspiring, and most women claim it was a fairy tale in the making. That was, until the whole truth was communicated and revealed. The woman that this man was so in love with had an excruciating life, a past full of shame, horror, heartbreak, sexual misconduct, abuse, and lies. Some might use words like *slut* or *whore* to describe her; others would use words like *abused* or *diseased*. Ultimately, there was just a whole lot of baggage and pain that had not been dealt with, ever.

Not to mention, this woman had tendencies of her old life even after she met this man. Though he loved her with all his heart, her former life of shame kept making its way into her speech, how she dressed, how others spoke to her, and even how she embraced her brand-new love. It was too heavy a burden for her, and something had to be done. Something had to be communicated.

On one particular occasion, she decided there could be no more secrets; there could be no more lies. This woman, who was broken as glass, came forth with every truth, every fear, all her insecurities, and more heartache than a nineties R&B artist. Her claim was that every man she ever had in her life either abused her or left her; either mistreated her or took advantage of her. She knew that this conversation left her more vulnerable than she had ever been. Her fears of being left again were in full force.

As my friend explained this story to me, he found himself in tears; his agony over her pain was just the beginning. Apparently, throughout their conversation, he wept more than she did.

He broke more than she had ever been broken, but he loved her more than she had ever been given. Though in part it killed him, his claim was that her past did not matter. It was their future he was interested in; his love was key to her destiny. So he chose to love her through it all. He chose to push his own pain aside and made the decision that the enduring force of love would save the day and ultimately her life.

Our Fairy Tale

My friends, this is *our* story. Thankfully, what seems to be a fairy tale is actually the truth: you and I represent the woman in this scenario, and Jesus Christ is the man. *This is how God loves the world, how he sees us all. He looks at the potential inside of us, not who we once were. God stood at the beginning of time and at the end, choosing to love us before our birth, during our sin, and after our redemption. We can only love him back because he loved us first.* It is because of this love he pursues us and sends us romance in the form of his Son. When no one else can love us, Christ can—and he does. He brings no pressure to us, only a gift of mercy. His mission is to tear down the walls of the hotel we have built in our hearts and rebuild a palace fit for two—you and the lover of your soul.

This Jesus wants to make us his bride, and our only chance of wearing white is to allow him to remove the stain of this hotel from our life's clothing. Christ gives you a direct definition of his relationship status with you. There are no other options for him; he sees no one else. *Christ's engagement ring to you was the price he paid on the cross. The wedding date is to be determined, but he is coming for a faithful and spotless bride.* He stands at your hotel door and knocks, saying that it is time to checkout! Only in his strength is this possible. This is the timeless truth that dominates despair. Christ the King wants you to know the victory of leaving the hotel, but Jesus the groom needs to be allowed into the room of your heart first. We just have to let him in.

As we move forward, I want you to know that my goal in all of this is not to offend you or force religion down your throat; it is simply to share my experiences and in doing so, help you find freedom from a hotel that may even seem like a prison. So, whether you are spiritual or agnostic, hopeful or hopeless, you will read proven truths inside the pages of this book that will apply to every area of your heart. My hope is that you will read with an open mind and let the rest take care of itself.

So, without further ado, I give you the Heartbreak Hotel.

Early Check-In

Growing up in Orlando, Florida, certainly had its benefits. Jumping in the car and going to the beach anytime you want is not something the majority of people in America get to do. When I was a child, my parents had a condo in New Smyrna, right on the beach. So it wasn't the Dominican, SoCal, or Australia, but what did I know other than the previous summers we spent at the Jersey Shore (which isn't exactly paradise). Anyway, this was the earliest I can remember going to a hotel, the first place I remember staying. I loved that place; they sold Yoo-Hoo chocolate milk in the vending machine, and they provided unlimited movie rentals at the front desk. Oh yeah, there were also poolside competitions during the day and a hot dog stand on the beach! I seriously loved that place, until that *dreadful day* …

I was young and in the kiddy pool; it started to storm, and I had all my toys in the water with me. If you have never lived in Florida, you probably don't understand the severity of our storms. They come at you fast and can strike quickly. This particular afternoon, the storm seemed to start out of nowhere. My mother was on the other side of the pool, and as it began to rain, she called for me to leave the water. In her Philly accent, she cried, "Huwwwry uuuuup, Jooooooe. Git outta tha wuter, *noooow!*" She made me leave all my toys in the water, never to be recovered. When we returned later, I was heartbroken to find that my toys were missing. Regardless of whether they were stolen or swept up by the storm, these were my regular and favorite toys, and losing them was instantly devastating.

Do you remember the first time you lost something valuable? Ponder that for a second. What might be insignificant to others could be treasure to you, or vice versa. It seems stupid to think that those instances could have created insecurities and fears on the inside, but it has for so many. Unfortunately, it can be the most minor experiences that force us to hold on to a lot of junk in life that we fear letting go of—stuff that really just needs to be released. Maybe something more tragic was taken from you and you have held on to it for years. Could that be the reason you have anger toward everyone for reasons you cannot explain? The vicious cycle started somewhere, and we are about to identify it.

My Personal Check-In

Okay, why don't we go a little deeper? This next story comes from an extremely vulnerable part of my soul. Before I go into it, please understand that throughout this book, you will read true stories that you might relate to. However, names may have been changed and certain details removed in my attempts to protect and honor anyone who has ever allowed me to incorporate their story into this book.

Have you ever had a friend who you loved and trusted? Sure you have. It is natural to show love and trust to people we appreciate. Well, this special friend was older than me; she had a really tough life, full of her own confusion and heartache. This early childhood friend of mine got checked into this hotel of heartbreak against her will, and worse, without understanding where she was going.

Let me pause here for a moment. See, once someone checks in to the hotel, they tend to bring others in with them. Some do it on purpose; others don't have a clue they are doing it at all—it just becomes natural. This is where I enter the scene with my friend. She didn't have a clue where she was taking me. *Prepare yourself for some intense content.* More than once, my friend, who I loved and trusted, violated my privacy. All you need to know is that she instructed me to do something with our bodies that I did not understand or even feel comfortable with. I trusted her and because I was extremely young, I did what she told me, without understanding that I too was checking into the Heartbreak Hotel.

So here we both were, doing ridiculous things that we didn't understand. The problem is, *just because we don't understand something does not mean it isn't destructive to our lives.* A parent's former pain checked her in and her newfound shame checked me in. And so the pattern of generational catastrophe continued. I don't pretend to claim that I was molested or raped, but I do know that this sat with me for years and has definitely affected my life and mind. The fact is that I am not alone in regards to this kind of experience. Sadly, some have known far worse. For me, I met disappointment and shame and it lingered for years … I checked in to Room 215.

When Did You Check In?

Does any of this sound familiar to you? Can you relate? Maybe your disappointment is more basic and practical. Maybe you were cut from your sports team or left out of a clique. Possibly, you were dumped, cheated on, or both. Maybe your pain is broader: divorce, abuse, addicted to drugs as a baby from pregnancy, it could be a learning disability, or some other struggle. Maybe the pain is both visible and invisible at the same time. A sixteen-year-old who has a baby. Someone suffering from obesity because of diseases that no one knows about. An individual with handicaps from something he did honorably, like serving his country. Hear me: I don't know what your pain is; what I do know is *your circumstance does not have to dictate your attitude, but your attitude will define your circumstance*. More importantly, *your circumstance is God's space to perform a miracle in your life*. So regardless of why, there is still a when: *when will you attain a win over this in your mind?* No matter the reason you checked in, your attitude determines the length of your stay, and your attitude is a function of the mind. The only way to conquer your circumstance is with an attitude adjustment, a 180-degree turn in your thinking. What you need is a complete renewal of the mind, a full-out transformation in thought patterns and thought focus (see Rom. 12:2). That sounds overwhelming, I know. At the same time, it absolutely can be done. Fortunately, you can start right now. Simply accept the statement: *things can be different.* Sit tight; we are getting there. I will show you how, step-by-step! Remember, the only goal in this first chapter is to identify the roots of our issues together, the reasons we checked in to the hotel in the first place.

Here are Your Room Keys

Indulge me for a moment as I tell you about my family. I am fortunate and blessed by heaven to have been given great parents. They made a lot of mistakes over the years, but they made them going at one hundred miles per hour, with all their heart. From them, I learned how to give, gain, and go toward my dreams. I am so thankful for that. I come from a family full of addiction, pain, fear, and disaster. Both sides of my family are from the Northeast, closer to the Philadelphia side of Pennsylvania. Not only does my family share heartbreak as we root for Philadelphia sports, we share it in the way most families have experienced pain. Your family and my family are really not all that different; we have all been affected by pain, but we are all just one or two decisions away from hotel checkout.

Before I share what is wrong, I must celebrate the things that are right. Both sides of my family would give the shirts off their backs. They would feed you, clothe you, house you, and befriend you. Just because they might have a broken heart, it doesn't mean their broken pieces aren't gold. So here is a very condensed version of my family.

Mom's side: My grandmother was violated and abused when she was younger and was without parents most of her life; then she met my grandfather and married him at the age of sixteen. My grandma never had time to heal through her childhood and became an avid drinker and an alcoholic. Thankfully, Alcoholics Anonymous played a huge role in saving her life. My grandfather is a unique man: he was a very hard worker and served his country well. He too grew up without a healthy home and it has most certainly made an imprint on his heart. Six kids and a miscarriage later, this family was surviving. My grandpa, who we call "Chick," worked hard through the years to provide; from night jobs to day jobs to side jobs to house jobs, he did it all for his family, faithfully.

No doubt, this family grew up in a dark time for our nation. *The sixties and seventies changed the way our nation stood, and instead, we began to lean. We started to lean on drugs and alcohol; we confused peace with tainted love.* I have witnessed two uncles pass away before their time, leaving wives and kids to cope. We have experienced our cousins, aunts, and uncles go in and out of jail, constantly on and off drugs. My family is victim to suicide, overdoses, and some major crime. It is difficult to write, but drugs, alcohol, and addiction have dictated more than forty years of our lives, resulting in fear, insecurity, hurt, bitterness, and distance. Even still, this family is resilient, and the movement out of the hotel of heartbreak is a daily process. It is happening, and it will complete its work sooner rather than later (see Phil. 1:6).

Dad's side: My father is quite a few years older than my mom, as he was married and had a life long before I ever existed. For your sake, I will limit his side of the story to just his first marriage and older kids. I have two half brothers and one half sister. It is a miracle that we are as close as we are—incredible to me how they have opened up their lives and let me in. My dad's first marriage did not work, and you can imagine the scars that this left on his children. Divorce is usually full of darkness, lies, blame, and crisis. I am sure all of those dynamics made their way into this situation too.

It takes years for healing, and sometimes it takes an entire lifetime. Today, I am proud to say that in both these families there is a sense of peace and wholeness forming. No question about it, nothing is perfect, nor will it ever be; yet all things become new when we allow for it (see Rev. 21:5).

I share these intimate details with you to illuminate some of the reasons *why* you might be in this hotel and *how* you were given these room keys. *One generation's insufficiencies will determine the next generation's tendencies.* Because of this, it is a natural process for us to walk the same lines, to potentially go down the same broken roads as our parents and grandparents. It will be our tendency to reenact or repeat failures of the past. The good news is that we don't have to. We do not have to live under these curses forever! Curses can be broken, and they can break with you. *You could very well walk out of this hotel, ensuring that your own children never walk in.* I cannot wait for my children to stand on my shoulders, much higher than I will ever go; they are going to be much stronger than I ever was. It is just my job to pave the way for them.

Up the Elevator and Down the Stairs

The first step in checking out of this hotel is to identify your issue. The second step is to identify where it started. I constantly watch heartbroken adults impart heartbreak on their children because they never identified the root of their problems. It isn't the bills or the stress of work or even the kids. These individuals walk around in chains without the knowledge of why and then blame it on things that are just by-products, easy excuses. *Sometimes our questions about the past overwhelm our opportunities in the present. We lose all perspective of what we have been given when we fail to identify what was taken.* The stories and circumstances you just read about are my identification processes. Now you must begin yours. I am confident that this is clearly speaking to you in some capacity. If so, identify whatever it is, call it out, and begin this checkout process!

Here is the other part: *where and when did pain and disappointment initially enter?* Think back as far as you can. This is going to hurt. You won't like this part; I certainly didn't. I found myself becoming angry with people, blaming them. This is an absolute *no-no!* This only enhances the pain and makes for additional nights in the hotel.

Right now, scenarios may be entering your mind—specific people and even specific geographical places rush to your brain. Deep warmth might surface in your body; blood temperature rises due to your remembrance. This is tough and you are not to blame for experiencing emotion. You do not want to go back and play in that kiddy pool anymore. It reminds you of disappointment, but *unfortunately your children and your future will feel the brunt of an unresolved past. We unintentionally disengage the next generation from innocence based off the perversion of our own experiences.* My ability to identify how I made the reservation at the hotel allowed me to cancel any future reservations. I knew where it was and what it was that checked me in, so I refused to keep the room once I was aware of the real cause of heartache.

Regardless of whether you have suppressed your pain into eternal forgetfulness, the reality is that it is still lingering somewhere in your fragile soul. No doubt, those experiences can—and, at times, should—be forgotten, but forgetting them without addressing them is only a set up for more painful confrontation later.

It is important to be careful and patient with ourselves during this process. We are unpacking emotional baggage that has been carried for a long time. Start slow and be easy about scratching and pulling at the stitches when the wounds are so fresh. Again, healing is beginning and it will be a process. Tomorrow is going to be better than today, and eventually, freedom from this painful past will reconcile us and build confidence in tomorrow. For example, time enables me to confess that just because I was violated by my friend yesterday does not mean I can't embark on new, healthy relationships today and tomorrow.

Channel Your Emotions

What now, you say? Well, I call it *emotion management.* Don't get too high and don't get too low. *Victory over heartbreak is found when we manage our emotions, rather than letting emotions manage us*. My suggestion is that you channel these unpredictable emotions differently. Try creating an outlet for them. What happens to us is that we don't know how to engage in healthy relationships, because our concept of health is skewed. *If we do not attain a victory over our past in our mind, then the people who try to love us in our present and future will pour into a bottomless cup.* So, *instead of holding onto anger, help those who have been hurt like you.* Maybe you can be a father, mother, sister, or brother to someone who has gone through divorce, because you know exactly what that is like. Maybe you can show love to an individual caught up in prostitution or illegal sex trafficking, because someone violated you. What if it were as practical as just being a friend to the friendless or feeding someone who was homeless?

For example, I don't always buy the nonsense that someone is "working on myself" right now, so they can't be involved in giving to and receiving from others' lives. *Your healing will normally come from a direct focus on someone or something other than yourself.* When you need a blood transfusion or an organ donation, the doctor goes into someone else to get it. *Additionally, your healing will always be connected to a healthy relationship*, like a healthy organ, a healthy heart, and healthy blood. Get it? *You have to let others in so that you can finally get out of your mess.* Take note, though: only let healthy others in, not those with the infected blood, erratic hearts, or blackened lungs. For me, I let a perfect God come in first and then I carefully let patient and giving people in next. This is *Healing 101*.

Checking out of this hotel is going to be harder than you think; it will be a process full of uncomfortable decisions. Ever heard the statement "It is going to get worse before it gets better"? It might feel that way for a while. *But*, it will get better, I promise. Oh, and congrats. You have now taken some huge steps toward checkout, maybe even the biggest steps you will need to take throughout this entire process.

–––––––––––––

Q 3s

These are questions that should initiate action. You may not be able to answer them in one sitting, but make them action items for your life.

1) Have you pinpointed exactly where and when you checked into the hotel?
   If you haven't or are having trouble, take some time and think about it.

2) Who is it that has disappointed and hurt you the most and why?

3) Where will you channel your emotions?

CHAPTER 2: **EXPLORING THE HOTEL (THE CHOICE CHAPTER/FOUR LEVELS OF BURN)**

We must embrace pain and burn it as fuel for our journey. -Kenji Miyazawa

Heavy first chapter, I know, but this is a heavy hotel that is full of heavy hearts. Life is so much lighter outside of these walls. On the outside, the burden is lifted; the load is much lighter to carry. You can do this, but we had to deal with the root issues first.

I remember being in the hotel, and as painful as it was, the more I explored the property, the more comfortable I became while staying there. Just like any hotel, though, it isn't and should never be home, and I got used to a room that I was never supposed to be sleeping in. As we explore, do not get comfortable!

Here we go. Let's dig into this next chapter as we break down our exploration of the hotel.

Nothing Wrong with a Little Mischief

When my parents moved from Philadelphia, we landed in a suburb of Orlando. We found a small neighborhood that was undergoing the beginning stages of development, just like my life. Fortunately for me, there was another young boy who lived down the street. Jamison, my very first friend, was about to check in to the Heartbreak Hotel, room 407.

It is funny that we even became friends. Maybe there weren't any other options. I say this because *rambunctious* is an understatement in regards to my demeanor back then. I was off the walls, a bull in a china shop, a firecracker—you get the point. Jamison was the complete opposite. He was as cool as the other side of the pillow.

All I know is, we were inseparable pals. Jamison and I would play Ninja Turtles together, ride bikes, and regularly get bullied by his older brother, Jordan. I have more scars on my body from Jordan than from all my years playing football.

Jamison would always go with us to our hotel at the beach during the winter and summer months. The first thing we would do is go exploring the hotel—our absolute favorite part! My Philly mother would always say, "Jooooooe, git owwwtta my hair; git inta some trouble somewhere else!!!" Neglected I was, completely (I'm just kidding)! So Jamison and I would search the joint up and down, find great lookout spots, and so on. After a while, exploration turned into mischief. We would knock on doors and run away as fast as we could. There were times when we would point laser pens at people to confuse them or leave "special gifts" when they answered the knock. We were high-grade criminals, let me tell you. During exploration, the worst thing that ever happened is that we broke the game room glass door with a pool ball. I mean, my mother did ask us to get into some trouble, right?

The First Guests

Now, before I give you the relevant part of the Jamison story, I need to set you up with an understanding of when and where the Heartbreak Hotel first opened. Almost everyone is familiar with the Bible story of Adam and Eve. These two individuals lived in a garden, representative of God's perfect plan for our lives. God told them plainly not to eat from the Tree of Knowledge of Good and Evil. He wanted them to steer clear of trouble or mischief. He desired for them to live a life that was free from continual heartache and misery. The same is still true for us today. God knows what is beneficial and harmful; his plan is that we experience a life free from constant pain. The sometimes-difficult part is that it is only accomplishable through obedience. Of course, the human element of exploration, usually leads to temptation. In our Bible story, there was a nasty snake. We will call him temptation. This snake was like a good bellhop; he helped them feel comfortable enough to settle in and unpack their first suitcase. After Adam and Eve gave in to temptation by eating from the tree, the snake then, without contention, carried their bags to their room—the place outside of the garden, which is the world that you and I know. It gets worse. The Bible says in Genesis 3:16–20:

> (God) said to the woman, "I will sharpen the pain of your pregnancy, and in pain you will give birth. And you will desire to control your husband, but he will rule over you." And to the man he said, "Since you listened to your wife and ate from the tree whose fruit I commanded you not to eat, the ground is cursed because of you. All your life you will struggle to scratch a living from it. It will grow thorns and thistles for you, though you will eat of its grains. By the sweat of your brow will you have food to eat until you return to the ground from which you were made. For you were made from dust, and to dust you will return."

Here's the Point

Painful pregnancy, stressful work, disease, poverty, hunger, and struggle have become regular visitors in this life we live. Believe it or not, though, it was never supposed to be that way. Can you imagine a practically painless pregnancy or even wealth without the need for employment? No, of course not. We have adapted; we've accepted the reality of this broken earth. Let me be most clear: I am not saying that there isn't good in the world today, because there most certainly is. *Where sin, shame, and sadness exist, there will also be just as much or more hope, opportunity, and grace* (see Rom. 5:20, author's paraphrase). Even still, one act of mischief or disobedience can send us on a tailspin crashing into the hotel lobby. Once we are there, we begin to get comfortable with our surroundings; we get comfortable in a place we aren't supposed to be. Adam and Eve accepted their fate. They existed in pain, and they invented their own death. Ultimately, they made their choice.

Even though Adam and Eve chose incorrectly, it doesn't mean you have to. God is asking you the same questions he asked them: *Will you listen to me? Will you trust that I have a plan for your life?* In the grand scheme of things, it doesn't matter if someone performed mischief on you or if you chose mischief yourself. There is a way to get back to the garden; there is a way to properly cope with and permanently fix any mistake that has been made. I have complete faith in your ability to do so, but connecting all of this together is key to our understanding of what to do next. It is obvious that we have some major decisions to make if we want to leave this hotel. Sometimes though, it can be difficult to make the right decisions when we are under pain and pressure. If you keep reading though, Jamison's story will illustrate our ability to reduce the pressure and choose a life inside the plan of the garden.

Exploring is Boring

For the first time, I experienced how one generation's heartache can trickle down to the next. One day, I went to Jamison's house and his parents were no longer together. *Divorce* was a new concept to me. I liked seeing his parents, and more than that, I loved having Jamison in the same neighborhood. After his parents split, Jamison moved out of the neighborhood with his mom and was not as accessible anymore. No doubt, heartache rippled through Jamison and his family. I cannot pretend to know all the details about his life, but I know Jamison had always been a blessing to me. *None* of this was ever his fault. It just was what it was; life happened and now he had to cope with his circumstances. I know how hard this was for him and his brother. Even as a kid, pain was wildly evident in his life. Some of you know what it's like to go back and forth between Mom and Dad's house. You are familiar with splitting holidays or watching your parents struggle financially, and then learning to navigate through their new relationships. Divorce was never part of the plan, but sadly, it stabs everyone connected in the gut ...

Eventually, most of us get used to the situation we are in, the pain of our past, the deck of cards we have been dealt. Jamison had a choice to make: what would he do about his circumstance?

Let me share the cool part of this story. Jamison refused to explore the hotel of heartbreak any longer. He decided that what he saw through his family was enough. For Jamison, *no hotel or former experience was ever going to keep him from an opportunity for love.* What is true about Jamison's life can be true for yours as well. Aren't you glad there is always an opportunity to make things right, even if you did not make them wrong in the first place? Thankfully, there is always redemption waiting on the other side of any missteps. I was fortunate enough to be part of Jamison's opportunity for love, his wedding day. What a beautiful ceremony, what a beautiful bride. The whole time, I could not help but think of how proud I was of him and how great life in the garden can be. Jamison made the right choice, will you?

From Pain to Promotion

Okay, why don't we shift gears and change our perspective a bit? I want to teach you something *good* about pain. You might think that all pain is bad, but burning pain as fuel for this journey is one hundred percent necessary. See, *there is a difference between hurting and burning. Both words reflect pain, but they are extremely different.* If I were to reference sports, we understand that *hurt* means you are sidelined, but *burn* might mean you are pushing, growing, getting stronger, and playing in the game. There is a necessary pain that should accompany your departure out of the hotel; that pain is your burn, just like when you work out—your legs, chest, and arms feel the burn. Living a life outside of the hotel and abiding in the plan of the garden requires the will to burn. That is why it is only after you burn that you will go beyond the walls of this hotel.

Healing takes courage. It takes courage to get off the bench, to test that injured knee, to disregard your past injury. That is exactly what Jamison did; he decided to burn his pain as fuel for the journey out of the hotel. Even though divorce caused his original example of love to fail, he chose to try love anyway. You can too. This choice promoted joy in his life, through the experience of his own marriage. *Pain can promise you promotion*, as long as you are willing to burn. My advice is that you stop exploring the dark and dreary rooms of this hotel. There is nothing here except for more of the same pain and trauma. Get out of the rut, make the choice and move past this rotten place. I urge you to stop exploring, resist temptation, and be obedient to whatever God is asking you to do. Believe me, he is asking you something; you have to decide what you are going to do with his voice …

Attention

Please note, the Heartbreak Hotel is not an easy place to leave; I think we have established that. Throughout our journey, I will implement practical steps that should make your departure easier. Additionally, these steps will be applicable for life outside the hotel too. My belief is that if you make these teaching points part of your lifestyle, you will build a strong defense against the sad army of misery. Below, we will discuss the first of these teaching points that I call, "The Four Levels of Burn."

The Four Levels of Burn

The opposite of death is life. The Heartbreak Hotel will steal life from you. If you want to live, you must fight every feeling inside that tries to get you to stay. To burn is to live life to the fullest. To burn properly, you must do one thing: *create a culture of LIFE* in everything you do, everything you say, and everywhere you go. *Let us burn so bright that our lives catch fire and blaze the door of this hotel wide open ...*

1) **L**ift someone up

Pick others up when they fall on difficult times. This will create both strength and character in you. Additionally, it builds bridges for when you need a friend. Think about it: putting someone on your shoulder burns your legs, but it also builds your influence, because people begin to trust that you can carry them. *You have the opportunity to go from heartbroken to hero.*

<u>Tips to Lift:</u>

Encourage people often.

Smile at someone.

Be available to others.

Think before you speak.

Ask appropriate, timely questions.

Speak to others the way you would want to be spoken to.

Look for the good in people rather than the bad.

2) Be Intentional about everything you do

Every decision has consequences; do not waste your time or life on things that have no lasting value. There will be times you have to walk away from situations or people. This might even mean that you lose friends and relationships. Your intentional decisions could actually save your life. In fact, I have heard it said that *your short-term decisions will govern your long-term goals*. What you do and decide today will absolutely matter tomorrow. Be intentional about what you decide!

Tips for being Intentional:

Forget regret.

Make your time in school count.

Be patient in your decision about your post high school plans.

Count the cost before you get into romantic relationships.

Make sure your friendships reflect your values.

Protect your time.

Manage your money wisely; you do not *NEED* everything.

3) Forgive yourself and others

Imagine a world in which people actually forgave themselves and those who have wronged them. Without a doubt, there would be less crime, pain, war, and sickness (yes, even sickness). A new world could be inspired by a united effort of creativity, honor, and outreach. Forgiveness unites differences in ideology, unlocking unlimited potential. Forgiveness equates to *power*.

This by far is the most important and most difficult element for gaining freedom from heartbreak. Hear me on this: *you cannot check out of the Heartbreak Hotel without forgiving yourself and others.* So, who is it you need to forgive?

Later on in the book, I am going to teach you a step-by-step process about forgiveness. Forgiveness starts with an initial decision, an initial willingness to get better. It is time to recognize who it is you need to forgive.

Tips to Forgive:

Choose to have patience with those who have hurt you.

Give second chances to those that do not deserve it.

Confess your pain to individuals like a professional counselor.

Practice letting things go.

Give yourself grace when you fail.

Talk about your past with those who you love and trust.

4) Endure 'til the end

Hardship, pain, and failure are just part of life. Get ready. At some point, it will find you. Vince Lombardi once said, "Life's battles don't always go to the stronger or the faster man, but sooner or later, the man who wins is the man who thinks he can." Finish strong, endure—you can do it!

An enduring people are the promise of a vibrant nation—economically, morally, and socially.

Tips to Endure:

Write down your dreams.

Talk about what you want to do with safe individuals who are willing to listen; network your goals.

Write down your plans and use a pros & cons method.

Practice discipline in the areas you are weak.

You are powerful, and by implementing some of these principles, you can be on your way to freedom! Let's keep moving on out of here.

————————

Q 3s

1) What is one decision you need to make after reading this chapter?

2) Is there someone or something in your past or present that keeps you from getting out of the hotel? If so, who or what is it?

3) Of the four levels of burn, which one do you need to focus on the most?

CHAPTER 3: **JUMPING ON THE BED**

No yesterdays are ever wasted for those who give themselves to today. -Brendan Francis

Do you remember the classic Christmas movie, *Home Alone?* The main character's name is Kevin, a little boy who is a huge pain in the backside. If you cannot remember the story line, his family leaves for vacation overseas, but they accidentally leave Kevin at home. In the morning, Kevin realizes that everyone is gone, so he runs upstairs and jumps on his parents' king-size bed. He jumps unabashedly, with no concern or fear for any of the potential consequences. He is even happy his family is gone! Later on in the movie, two goofball criminals harass him, and even though he outsmarts them, by the end of it, he realizes there are consequences to jumping on the bed and being home alone.

Boy oh boy, this scene illustrates our lives in a direct way. Certainly, you have jumped on the bed at a hotel before, right? How could you not? Probably the most fun part about being in a hotel room is jumping on a bed that isn't yours. This feels carefree—no rules and no consequences. Well, until something breaks, of course. Many of us have gotten to this point in our lives; we are so comfortable with the mess and the pain we are in that we lose all sense of responsibility, passion, conviction, and discernment. Things begin to break; we get more in debt to sin, pain, and struggle. But sooner or later, jumping on the bed gets boring and we are left leaning over the balcony, headed toward self-injury and even death. Like Kevin, life without rules can be a party. That is, until the party ends and reality sets in. You should ask yourself, is the party starting to end? Has reality blindsided me? If so, the answers for hope are not all that complex. It is simply time for a dose of purpose, rules, and protection. These power keys will give you the strength to finally get off this bed and take hold of a life you were always intended to have ...

Self-Deceived

I have been so fortunate to travel to over fourteen different countries in my short life thus far. I have seen more in my youth than some have gotten to see their entire lives. I say none of this to brag but rather to celebrate the blessed life I have been given. With that said, there are few places as classic and as beautiful as Vienna, Austria, or even as romantic as the Spanish cities of Madrid and Barcelona. I could tell you about the see-through water at the Dominican beaches and the centuries-old castles in Ireland. Have you ever stood in an ancient cathedral in Europe? It will take your breath away! How about a WWII memorial? Or have you simply tasted a waffle from Belgium? Wow, this world is absolutely full of beautiful sites, glorious landscapes, and incredibly tasty treats.

On the other hand, I have also stood in homes that we would consider poor excuses for our tool sheds in the mountains of Nicaragua. I have delivered food and resources to naked, dirty children living in neglected Romanian villages in Ukraine. I have watched little children beat each other with metal bats just to get to a piece of candy. A lot of people who live in this world cover their trauma with so much makeup that no one can tell how ugly their situation really is. Nations do this, governments do this, and, yes, even churches do this. These incredible nations that I have visited all have this in common. They wear so much makeup, but there is actually significant ugliness at the core. This core I speak of has nothing to do with the natural beauty of the people, their culture, or their customs. The ugliness comes from what they choose to accept and overlook. Some actually accept oppression, abuse, or even lies and manipulation. It is almost as if the bed is given, so why not jump on it?

This even goes for the United States, which absolutely pains me to say. You won't find a more proud American than me, but I do recognize the plastic surgery and easy fixes we have used to cover up our real issues. Make no mistake; we have real moral inefficiencies, which are carried over into our economic and social situations. This is a generational problem. It is not only my generation, but the generation before me as well. Even our recognized leaders have indulged in selfishness and irresponsibility. We have serious ethical injustices taking place, and worse than that, we have a lot of "do what I say, not as I do" going on. Our nation *was not* built on compromise; it was built on sacrifice. The same will go for checking out of this hotel of ours.

At the core, jumping on the bed is an act of selfishness. We use our pain as an excuse to indulge in unhealthy behaviors. This is why some of us cut ourselves or sleep around, abuse drugs and live in depression. We think we are excused to fail and by doing these things, it will cover up the real pain. Then we get angry and wonder why we have acquired diseases and unwanted pregnancies. *This is never acceptable and not good enough!* In the next section, you get to meet a young lady who was willing to exchange excuses for purpose. She answers our questions as to whether jumping on the bed is sustainable, acceptable, or downright disastrous.

Edge of Desire

Meet Jenna from Atlanta, room 706. As a pastor's kid and smart girl, Jenna had a life full of opportunity and potential. Unfortunately, Jenna was checked in to the Heartbreak Hotel way too early in life. Prior to becoming a pastor, Dad was on the road constantly for business while Mom was a housewife. Jenna was young but understood something was not right. As Dad traveled, the marriage crumbled due to infidelities and neglect. As Jenna describes, it was obvious that her father wanted money and status more than he wanted his family. At the same time, she tells me that her mom never wanted to partner with her dad on his goals either. Those combining factors put a strain on the entire family.

If you talk to Jenna today, she will tell you that every man in her life has disappointed her, and that she has feared being left since childhood. You can already tell that an enormous amount of insecurity was building inside this young lady's heart, regardless of her family's status as "church folk." Eventually, Jenna grew tired of feeling empty and alone, so she began to pursue excitement as a distraction from the rip in her heart. You can probably predict where this story is going. Jenna began to engage in a variety of unhealthy behaviors. There was binge drinking, out-of-control partying, multiple sexual partners, and extremely dangerous activity—Jenna's life was spinning way out of control.

Here's the kicker: Jenna grew up with a set of moral principles and Christian values that had been instilled in her since childhood. These values were set in place for protection, for her future. She will tell you that she thought she really believed in these principles. What happened, though, is such a classic case: *she based her values on theory rather than experience.* When your beliefs about spirituality and principle are just theory, you will abandon them when life gets difficult. Jenna began to have really tough times, *and because her foundation was shaky, she couldn't stand out. Instead, she blended in.*

Now that Jenna had blended in, she got comfortable going with the flow, doing what everyone else was doing. She was literally jumping on the bed of irresponsibility and carelessness. All those around her were merely coping with their pain by numbing it with falsified love and adrenaline. Unfortunately, the longer people jump on this bed, the less careful they will be not to break anything. I remember one instance when I was jumping back and forth from bed to bed in our hotel room and landed on the nightstand. Not only did the nightstand break, but also a chunk of my head too! Blood and pain, blood and pain! And so it goes with our lives. *We jump and jump, getting riskier and less careful about our principles, and the next thing you know, we break and are left hurt and ashamed, lost and bleeding on the inside.*

So what happened to our friend Jenna? Well, the same thing that may have happened to you. Jenna found herself near the edge, standing on the balcony of the hotel. Remember, this was once a happy and passionate young lady, full of hope and promise. Now, she is considering a final end to all her pain—at least this is what she thinks death will bring her. It is so sad because this could not be further from the truth. I am not here to ram religion or theories down your throat, but I did write this book to help free you. The truth is, there is a post-death life, a two-way street. One side of the street leads to gold walkways and crystal waters, eternal rest. The other side leads to a multiplication of your already broken-hearted isolation. *There is a catch:* the beginning of the two-way street looks completely opposite of the end outlook. The road to life and freedom is narrow and full of that burn we talked about in the previous chapter. The road to death is very easy to walk down—extremely wide and lacking any burn. To leave the hotel, you've got to do what's unnatural, and you have to burn. *Suicide and self-injury involves no burn. It's what's easy, not what's right.*

The Long Road Home

Though the narrow road is difficult, the lasting opportunities are significantly better. Thankfully, *whenever there is crisis, there is opportunity* to change course. I am not suggesting that one should force crisis to initiate opportunity, but I am declaring that mercy still exists on this planet, and I intend to receive it; you should too. As Jenna told me her story, she used words like *hurt, used, gross, embarrassed, broken, abandoned, alone, stranded*, and *hopeless*. She also used words like *found*, *saved*, *maturity*, *whole*, *hopeful*, *freedom*, *changed*, *peace*, and *contentment*. Her latter words were quite different from her former words. It is easy to write these words from my perspective, but it was not easy for her to attain them, not at all. Jenna had to make major changes; she had to burn.

Jenna did three significant things that pushed her from the room to the lobby, the lobby to the parking lot, and finally the parking lot to her home.

1) <u>She put her theory to the test:</u> For Jenna, her belief in Christianity had to be tested. She could not live off sermons anymore; she had to see if this Jesus thing was actually real. She humbled herself, got on her face, and cried out to a true, living God. She wept and pleaded and was willing to sit at the feet of this God until she knew him for herself, until it was personal. Her story reminds me of the prodigal son; Jesus tells this brilliant story in the Gospel of Luke 15:11–32. Long story short, there was a young son who wanted to experience the world for himself, so he asked for his inheritance and left. Throughout his travels, all the parties and pain, he found that the road wasn't all it was cracked up to be. Eventually he came running home in hopes that his father would take him back into his house. He did not care if he was taken back

as a son or as a servant. The good father, of course, receives him as his son and throws a party in his honor.

The awesome thing about the prodigal son and Jenna's story is that it is really the same for you and me today. The very second Jenna started to come home; her Heavenly Father met her with open arms. At that point, she fell to her face and wept at his feet. The reason she wept and stayed at his feet so long is because she finally realized it was all the adrenaline, excitement, love, and security that she had been searching for her whole life. That is why *education without experience is useless!* Unless you find out if what you believe is actually true, you toil to educate yourself for no reason at all.

YOUR APPLICATION: I am not sure where you stand on spirituality or values, but my suggestion is that whatever your beliefs are, put them to the test; find out if they are actually real. If you believe in nothing, you will fade; you may eventually even die for a lack of vision and purpose (see Prov. 29:18).

2) <u>Jenna removed her distractions:</u> I am not the guy who will preach against dating and relationships. In fact, I vouch for them. Of course, my vying for your relationships is based on your healthiness (later in the book, we will break down seven key relationship deal-breakers). Family brought about Jenna's initial hurt, but her distraction came

from guys. Eventually, that drove her desire to be accepted by her peers, leading to partying, abuse, and more painful disaster. With these constant grenades in her life, her health could blow up at any moment. Jenna's safety rested in her willingness to burn for a time. Sometimes you have to be willing to be alone. You will find out really quickly who your true friends and family are, who truly loves you. It is the safest place to be for a short time, as long as you don't stay secluded forever. This is exactly what Jenna did: she got stronger. As it always happens, the proper relationships have been handed to her in time. Her victory is supported by her daily decisions to stay on the narrow road.

YOUR APPLICATION: Let me take this time to speak to addictions for just a moment. I will use my aunt as an example. Let me just say how proud of her I am. My entire life, this aunt has acted more like a younger sister than an older aunt. She has been in and out of jail, on and off of drugs, and, worse, inconsistently in and out of our lives. Here is a woman nearing her fifties and still battling demons dating back to her birth. My aunt is an expert on addiction. She will tell you all about how it ruins lives, destroys relationships, and shatters your identity. She has never been able to be the mom, the aunt, the sister, or the daughter she has wanted to be. Even still, she has battled especially hard lately. This woman is taking ground she has never taken. I think she is finally ready to check out of that hotel. *But*, like Jenna, she had to remove the distractions. She had to put away the old and embrace the new. She had to stop drinking metaphorical milk and begin to eat solid food; she had to humble herself and check into rehab; she had to give up money and embrace thrift. Such is true for us. We must strip off what holds us down and holds us back and keep the main thing, the main thing—this being the healthiness of our lives.

The destruction of addiction rests in the construction of healthy habits. What kind of habits are you forming right now? No one says it better than Ralph Waldo Emerson: "Watch your thoughts. They become words. Watch your words. They become deeds. Watch your deeds. They become habits. Watch your habits. They become character. Character is everything."

3) <u>She became consumed by purpose</u>: I am an unabashed believer in the local church. Okay, let me restate: I am an unabashed believer in the *healthy* local church. Too many people have terrible ideas of what the church is and should be. Jenna was fortunate to have been able to engage in a community where purpose was dripping off the walls. Jenna got involved immediately at an organization that works directly with crisis prevention. Like we touched on in

Chapter One, channeling your emotion is absolutely necessary for continual survival outside of the hotel. This is exactly what Jenna did. *Freedom is found in identity. Simply put, without identity, we are like illegal aliens, existing without the benefits of kingdom citizenship.* Jenna applied for an ID in the Kingdom of God, and she has been reaping the benefits of being a citizen for Jesus ever since. She is learning whose she is, where to go, and what to do; that is what I call purpose!

YOUR APPLICATION: What are you good at? What are you passionate about? Do everything you possibly can to expend your energy on things that matter, on building lasting bridges. This way, you will be able to stand firm on a solid foundation, whenever it is you are feeling weak. This is not limited to spiritual or crisis management organizations. Some of us just need to go be on a sports team, go to the gym, take up a healthy hobby, or even make some friends who have the same values as us. Proper exercise will always result in proper growth in regards to your goals. It is absolutely necessary for you to set personal goals for your life and for your future. If you aren't reaching for any stars, you will certainly never attain anything above your head. C'mon, defy some gravity on this planet; get a firm grip on purpose!

I sure hope you are ready to get off of this bed. I certainly don't want to jump on it anymore! Let's go! Chapter Four, here we come!

——————————

Q 3s

1) What do you believe about spirituality and the existence of God?

2) Can you identify with Jenna? If so, in what ways?

3) Do you have any addictions in your life? If so, with whom are you going to talk to?

(PART 2 – ROOM SERVICE)

CHAPTER 4: **BILL MY ROOM (HIGHWAY TO THE DANGER ZONE)**

God brings men into deep waters, not to drown them, but to cleanse them. -John Aughey

1986—remember that year? Some of you weren't even a thought; others, well, you were already thinking about way too much. Either way, this was an extremely interesting year in our world.

The year started out with a bang, literally. Most people remember how the *Challenger* space shuttle exploded on the twenty-eighth of January, an extremely sad day for the world and especially America. All seven of our astronauts, including a schoolteacher, died seventy-three seconds into the launch. Heartbreak? You better believe it.

Hands Across America, in which I participated, also took place in 1986. My family actually has a video of it. I was only three and a half months old. At least five million people formed a human chain from New York City to Long Beach, California, to raise money to fight hunger and homelessness. Awesome! Well, that obviously gives away the fact that the most important birth in the history of the world took place in 1986 as well—mine! Okay, hardly the most important, but just laugh with me!

One of pop culture's more famous 1986 moments comes from the classic movie *Top Gun.* There is a classic theme song that goes with it, which the subtitle of this chapter comes from: "Danger Zone," by Kenny Loggins. I have to show you some lyrics from the chorus:

Chorus:

"Highway to the Danger Zone

Gonna take it right into the Danger Zone

Highway to the Danger Zone

Ride into the Danger Zone"

Unfortunately, too many folks live by a very dangerous code in a life-threatening zone. This is a place where the safety of a movie set in Hollywood does not exist. It is one thing to take risks and have faith for your dreams; it is another to live between a burning fire and a shark-infested tank. When we live in this dangerous zone, a painful death is almost guaranteed to ensue. That is why the next two chapters are going to deal with a specific word that plagues the likes of pupils, politicians, preachers, pastors, and parents. This word is not to be played with; it ruins married folks and single people alike. The word I am referring to is *lust*. That's right, the other L word. There is more to lust though than just sexuality; lust deals with one's eyes, skin, and heart. Certainly, sexuality plays a huge role in regards to lust, but individuals also lust for way more than sex. There is the lust for *more*: more money, more things, more territory, more this, and more that. In this chapter, we will focus on lust from a sexual perspective. In the next chapter, we will dive into the lust for more. By the way, it should be obvious to you that lust is the danger zone. Lust can and will end you; it is that serious. So, here we go. Hold on tight!

Advertisements

Ever passed a hotel and noticed their advertisements for free channels or free wireless Internet? This always attracts me to their hotel because if I have my laptop with me, I can always work from my room (on my fantasy football team).

A few years back, when I was playing college football, we were traveling to a game and stayed in a hotel in Topeka, Kansas. God bless the Midwest, but something was extremely eerie about Topeka that night, just spooky. Worse, the hotel we stayed at was quite possibly the nastiest hotel of all time. The mattresses were as thin as paper and had stains all over them; the bathrooms smelled, and the TV was about nine inches tall. It was just awful. By now, you guessed it; I didn't play Division 1 or FBS ball—more like high school ball that provided scholarships. Anyway, with all that said, there was wireless Internet, our only consolation. You could say that there was nothing we wanted to do more then get the heck out of there. Please, Coach, *check us out of here!* This kind of hotel seemed to be standard for our travels during football season. Certainly you understand why: the price. These hotels were advertising cheap rooms and Internet, and our program claimed they couldn't afford the Marriot, so we slept somewhere between death and the jungle every time we went on the road. You could call me a warrior of sorts—a road warrior!

Sadly, this is the revelation of so many of our lives. We are on the road of life, going about our business, searching for purpose, holding out for love, until the advertisements distract us. These advertisements sink us, draining us of all our energy, and eventually we just drown. As we gasp for our final breath, we land in a weird, scary place like the hotel above. It isn't what's best for our lives, not even what's good. It is simply settling for cheap rather than getting the reward of a price well paid. *Lust seems to steer our wheel toward cheap trash while we have Daddy's unlimited credit card to spend on the penthouse of promise.* Please believe me, lust serves as a deterrent, a complete distraction. Like I have mentioned before; you belong inside the safety of God's plan. There is a purpose and a mission for your life. I would hate for you to be distracted from your appointment with destiny because if you live distracted, you won't ever make it. With that said, what are some distractions for you? Throughout this chapter, list a few you struggle with, and feel free to take your time. As you begin spanning your heart, I will direct you to some solutions that Christ provides for this common distraction of lust. Let's continue …

That's Expensive

Remember that Jesus character I just mentioned to you? He is going to take over for a moment because this subject is so close to his heart. Here is one of his stories:

Meanwhile, the disciples were in trouble far away from land, for a strong wind had risen, and they were fighting heavy waves. About three o'clock in the morning Jesus came toward them, walking on the water. When the disciples saw him walking on the water, they were terrified. In their fear, they cried out, 'It's a ghost!' But Jesus spoke to them at once. 'Don't be afraid,' he said. 'Take courage. I am here!' Then Peter called to him, 'Lord, if it's really you,

tell me to come to you, walking on the water.'
'Yes, come,' Jesus said. So Peter went over the
side of the boat and walked on the water toward
Jesus. *But when he saw the strong wind and*
the waves, he was terrified and began to sink.
'Save me, Lord!' he shouted (Matt. 14:24–30).

Our friend Peter gets distracted from the goal
here; he starts to sink in the advertisements.
The wind and waves are so representative of our
culture today; they are just one element of the
advertisements and distractions. Jesus represents
everything that is good, everything that is right.
For example, let's just say Jesus represents
proper, healthy relationships between a man and
a woman. The wind and waves play a distracting
role, and instead of man and woman, we see it as
man and man or a woman and woman. For some,
difficult to stomach, I get that. Still, sexuality was
originally never intended to be outside of marriage,
and marriage was intended to be between a man
and a woman. Wind and waves have gotten to our
humanity, our culture, and our world. Heartbreak
has seeped through generations and has distorted
truth. *Every time someone is molested, abused,*
abandoned, or lied to, his vision becomes blurred
and his mind becomes indoctrinated incorrectly.
Sexual misconduct and violation do awful things
to the body, but worse things to the mind. Some
get impregnated with babies, but most get
impregnated with impure ideas. Through all this,
Jesus still stands on the water, perfect, waiting for
us to just look up.

This Christ who stands on the water represents his perfect rescue to you and perfect destiny for *you*. Most of us dream of getting married, having a family, and accomplishing something meaningful on this planet. Here is another example of why lust is so detrimental:

Media, pornography, and a sexually obscene society have completely distorted our vision. These entities have literally taken the salt water from the waves and splashed it into our moral eyes. Those who call pornography art try to rub paint so deep in our eyes that all we can see is a distorted image of what used to be pure. So instead of seeking out a woman for her soft heart, gentle spirit, working hands, and natural beauty, we have been trained to long for plastic perfection. Ladies, since when did naked firemen or Abercrombie models become more attractive then security, integrity, and hard work? Some people literally are not attracted to anything other than airbrushed pornography, computer-generated fantasy models. This is not representative of a real, tangible human being. *Some of us hate our reality so much that we create our own fantasies that numb us from the disastrous regularity we live in.* Make a choice today: live in truth and embrace what you have been given, not what can be manipulated.

Now, before you decide I'm crazy, let me fully clarify. There is nothing wrong with having a sex drive; there is nothing wrong with desiring specific parts on or qualities in the opposite sex. The problem occurs when you are the one driving the car. Just sit on the passenger side and *let this perfect Christ drive you to his flawlessly timed sexual destination for your life.*

I trust you are getting this. *Just like any sort of room service is expensive, operating in the danger zone of lust is extraordinarily costly. In fact, it will empty your bank account, ruin your retirement, eat up your pantry, and put you on the spiritual welfare line.* For some, it takes their jobs, their homes, and can even rob them of their future. It drives some individuals to such depths of selfishness that they destroy their families, friends, and their children's futures. Ouch. This reminds me of the author James, from the Bible. He writes in his fourth chapter, verse one:

> What is causing the quarrels and fights among you? Don't they come from the evil desires at war within you? You want what you don't have, so you scheme and kill to get it. You are jealous of what others have, but you can't get it, so you fight and wage war to take it away from them. Yet you don't have what you want because you don't ask God for it. *And even when you ask, you don't get it because your motives are all wrong—you want only what will give you pleasure* (Italics mine).

This verse makes me think of a well-known political scandal of a former congressman. If you are not familiar, he got caught sending nasty direct messages through Twitter to a variety of women. He lied to the media and tried to cover it up, but it eventually blew up in his face. What is so interesting is the drama it caused throughout the nation and world. We quarreled, we fought, we argued, and in some ways, his indiscretions divided Washington. Should he stay, should he go? Furthermore, his wife was in her early stages of pregnancy with their first child. They say he could have run for president one day. Do you get where I'm going with this? Lust is a destructive force to all it comes in contact with. It distracted the congressman from doing his part to serve his country, it potentially derailed his marriage, it caused uproar within our media, and it diminished what could have been an esteemed life of public service. That's why lust is very *expensive!* Do not underestimate it.

There are a few things that I have been taught and a few things I have discovered about defeating the distractions of untimely sexuality; this I need to share with you. It wouldn't be fair if I kept them all to myself. That certainly wouldn't help check you out of this hotel; and of course, that is absolutely what I am here to help you do. Take a look at these key teaching points about defeating distractions:

Defeating Distractions

Let's go back to Matthew 14:30: *"But when he saw the strong wind and the waves, he was terrified and began to sink"* (Italics mine). You have to look up and away from those advertisements. Ignoring the wind and waves takes major discipline.

Here are some steps:

1) Have Discipline in Your Mind

There are various songs and quotes by writers that say things like "My mind says no, but my body says go!" or "My heart's telling me no, but my body is telling me yes!" This is both clever and true. There is a reason their hearts and minds tell them no first. Sex is a blessing; it is a necessary growth and connection point for married couples. Those lines above reflect an understanding that sexual engagement before its protected vault of marriage complicates things and damages lives. This is any sort of sexual engagement, by the way, *not just intercourse.* The reason this is such a distraction point is because our culture doesn't see it this way. Instead of being celebrated for your celibacy, you are mocked. Instead of being honored for your intelligent avoidance of potential heartbreak, you are pressured to test-drive a variety of vehicles, a variety of people. I beg you, don't make this mistake. Decide that lust isn't going to rule over you. Be different than your peers and even your world, because someone, somewhere, is preparing to be your wife or husband. Hold out for them; stay faithful even before you meet them. One day, you will have a beautiful gift to offer your spouse.

I really believe in your desire to be different, to stand out. At the same time, *don't tell me you want something different for your life, but do the same things as everybody else.* If you do the same things, but expect different results, you are insane. I dare you to go against the flow. If you do, you will know every angle, both the good and the bad. At that point, your knowledge of the harm will almost make the right choices for you. Trust me; you do not want to be another statistic.

Food for thought: We live in a culture that is, at times, brainless. Teachers have sex with students, eleven-year-olds get pregnant, and our World Wide Web has websites offering child pornography. If we don't protect our minds with truth, then it is over; we are going to sink. This is why the mind must be disciplined, why the mind must be renewed. This is why the mind must be exercised with both intellect and spirituality. For this to work, it requires a mindset readjustment. You have to know, your world does not think like this (see John 15:19). Retrain your mind to think differently by replacing negative thoughts with powerful Scriptures. Speak to your negative emotions with authority and shut off all doubt that you are meant for more than this hotel. Your mind is a gift, practice protecting it.

2) <u>Have Discipline in Your Body</u>

Hopefully everyone knows that it isn't enough just to work out. One must eat right too. You cannot have the lifetime six-pack without the daily effort. The apostle Paul said this:

I discipline my body like an athlete, training it to do what it should. Otherwise, I fear that after preaching to others I myself might be disqualified (1 Cor. 9:27).

Whether you are a leader, minister, student, or young adult, you never, ever want to be disqualified in this race of life. You belong. So stay in your lane and be disciplined enough to run full speed without crossing over into someone else's. This definitely applies to your sexuality.

I was speaking at a music festival a while back and was walking through the merchandise tent, looking for some gear. Unfortunately, my heart and mind went to another place when I stumbled upon the resource table of a particular abstinence organization. The table was filled with statistics of the problems caused by premarital sexual engagement. There was one chart in particular that really broke my heart. It wasn't the chart about sexually transmitted diseases or the chart about the issues relating to homosexuality. The chart that really got to me was the one that showed the multiplication of sexual partners you have when you sleep with more than one person. For example, the chart claimed that if you sleep with four people in your life, it is equivalent to sleeping with fifteen. Ouch! This is an excruciating statistic, especially when you find yourself in love, or more important, when you meet the person you are going to marry. You will want to offer your husband or wife yourself and yourself alone, not twenty other people. Please believe that there is hope for those who have fallen into this trap. In fact, I believe that your body, mind, and heart can be completely restored. I believe God can and does restore virginity, but only if you live out this new life of discipline (see 2 Cor. 5:17).

This is why singles must stay the course of purity and abstinence; your time is coming when you will get to run in the relays, but for now, keep running toward the prize that is waiting for you. For married folks, you are blessed enough to be on a team; don't forget that. There is no better team for you than the one you are already on. Win with that team! That is what keeping your eye on the prize is all about ...

As I talk with students or even friends, the question always arises: "What am I supposed to do with this sex drive until I get married?" Or someone says, "Man, pray for me because I need God to limit my desire for sex." This is always funny to me because I don't want God to take my sex drive away, whether I am married or not. I just want God to give me the grace to continue on and be disciplined enough to position myself for success.

At the same time, it is definitely necessary to talk about sex and our struggles in a confident, safe place. When communicating this subject, remember that it is both normal and necessary. First, talking about sex can sometimes be awkward for people—it can be difficult to communicate, and communicate properly. So relax and know that this is helpful for your future and is beneficial to talk about. Second, and most important, don't ever pray for a decrease or removal of your sex drive. God gave it to you; God is not a dad that takes his gifts back. So, let me repeat: sex is healthy, necessary, and important.

The prayer should be about timing and discipline. I have heard it said that men are stimulated by sight and women are stimulated by what they hear. Whether that is true or not, your eyes and ears are two body parts that need major discipline. These areas are gateways right to your heart. If you protect the things you let your eyes see, I guarantee you will be less apt to search for something that isn't real. I will even take an unscientific guess that we can eliminate a large percentage of our lust issues by eliminating just half of what we watch through our media outlets. The same goes with our ears. Sometimes when I am speaking somewhere, I will read lyrics of a few songs from the top ten radio hits of the day. It is a funny exercise, but I make my point because I can barely get through half the songs. What happens is that most of the audience is singing right along with my reading. Because the songs are obviously dirty, harmful, and almost embarrassing to read, my sarcasm takes over. My point is well taken; *how can what comes out of us be whole, when what goes inside of us is broken?* This is essentially what is taking place when we put trash in our ears; trash will come out through our mouths and influence the temperature of not only our own lives, but the lives of others as well.

In addition, when it comes to your protection, what you wear and where you go matters too. Ladies get the brunt of this subject, sometimes unfairly. Certainly, women should and can protect men by what they wear. Ladies, sometimes it feels like I am at the beach when I'm really just at the mall. As a woman, you have a responsibility to dress in a way that protects your body and earns you respect from both men and women. Doing this will also serve as protection for boys and men who are trying to keep their purity and abstinence intact.

At the same time, guys, wearing sexually explicit T-shirts doesn't do anything but heighten your sexual psyche. As a man, you are not exempt from this responsibility to dress appropriately either. In fact, you must lead the way! Create your own personal expectations for the women you surround yourself with. Don't date or marry a woman if you're uncomfortable with the way she dresses.

I lived in Vienna, Austria, for a few months. In Europe, you walk quite a bit, and I loved that, but every time I walked to church, I passed a strip club. The club was right on the corner, practically next to the church. Great location! Seriously. Everybody, from pastor to congregant, noticed the club. If I ever popped into the club and surrounded myself with that culture of sex, I would most certainly be inclined to act on it. This wouldn't be out of a desire to self-destruct, but out of a habit, out of a natural tendency to do what I see, to become what I've surrounded myself with. It's the same concept with clubs, certain bars, and other sexually tense venues. What you might find ridiculous today could save your life tomorrow. I pray you are willing to *do the difficult things now and receive the eternal rewards later.*

Food for thought: Build a filter and monitor within your heart and spirit. That is all discipline is; it's staying inside the lines you have drawn for yourself. Here are some things that I have done throughout my life to protect my body:

Replaced negative music with positive praise and worship.

I put a program on my computer that sends emails to a few people if I go to questionable websites.

I stayed away from certain atmospheres where alcohol and drugs were prevalent.

Abstinence.

3) Have Discipline in Your Time

In Craig Groeschel's book, *WEIRD*, he talks about protecting yourself by the positions you put yourself in or the positions you keep yourself out of. He gives one suggestion that four feet should always stay on the ground. I like that! He means if two unmarried people are sitting on the couch together, they should keep both feet on the ground. That will keep the two people from lying on each other and more. By the way, sometimes I feel like this book is a little bit weird anyway because these concepts are so countercultural. In fact, I say that *Christianity will always flow counter-culturally*. Maybe you're reading this book and you don't claim Christianity or any form of spirituality at all. Know that these principles are universal, and they are timeless protections for your life. The reason I reference Christ so much is because he was such a revolutionary; a wealth of knowledge for the fragile heart. I don't know who he is for you, but for me, he is my plan A of protection from this hotel. I have no plan B; Christ is my all in all, he is my life.

So, what does that have to do with disciplining your time? So glad you asked. If you want to protect your heart, soul, and life from the hotel of heartbreak, then you will be ever conscious of who gets your time and when they get it.

I had a friend who used to come to me often and share with me his struggles and heartbreak. He used to tell me that his parents were so messed up: Dad watched pornography and drank all the time, and Mom was crazy. He felt like these violations were passed right down to him. His claim was that he couldn't control himself with women because it was in him. Maybe this is true. Maybe his lack of discipline was a generational curse, but even still, I was interested in his patterns. Sure enough, he always hung out with his girlfriends very late at night and at home by himself. If you get two sexually charged people in a room alone, especially late at night, I can guarantee that eventually something will happen.

So instead, be intentional about the time you spend and with whom you spend it. Spend time in healthy venues, date in public rather than at home alone all the time, and give your time to purposeful, lasting things. This could be church, volunteering with non-profits, feeding the homeless, or building your community. Invest your time in things that last. That way, your legacy and reputation will remain long after you are gone.

Food for thought: Disciplining your time is quintessential in your survival. Though listed number three, it could easily rank at number one. Keep your time protected so you can keep your future selected at your own will, not by unwanted circumstances.

4) Have Discipline in Your Relationships

What's most important is the discipline it takes to wait for the right relationships. I am not going to harp on this for very long, because I will dip into relationships in a couple of chapters; here I will briefly illustrate it:

Isn't it every man's lifetime goal to marry a Dallas Cowboy cheerleader? Okay, I am being facetious, but I presume that those cheerleaders are still the world's most famous sex symbols. For a while there, I too was convinced that I was marrying into the family of Cowboys cheerleaders. Not sure where I got this idea, but at some point in high school, I was hoping for miracles bigger than any ocean parting or sun standing still. With that said, there is probably a good majority of those cheerleaders who live an incredibly wholesome, moral life. I am not trying to bash those ladies. This statement is to simply remind both you and myself of what is important. *Our motives for relationships will predetermine our discipline once involved in them*. Who we choose to be in relationships with can set off a variety of bombs for our life. On the other hand, it can also surround us with a variety of healthy, protective shields. My motive for wanting to marry a cheerleader was based off of shallow sexuality, not intellectual and spiritual depth. Maybe if I met one of those ladies, it would be different, but my motives were way off. I would have been walking into the relationship improperly because I know them as sex symbols, not as real people.

It is so important for us to maintain perspective in acquiring any type of relationships. Do you want particular friends for status? Do you want a romantic relationship to fill a void? Is it impossible for you to ever be single? Unless you have the discipline to say no to these questions, you won't have discipline to protect yourself once you are in the actual relationships. Be careful and find a way to live a disciplined life ...

Food for thought: There is no rush for relationships, no matter the age. This is the greatest piece of advice I could give throughout any part of this book. It is probably better to be single and wishing you were involved than to be involved and wishing you were single. Solomon in the Bible tells us to never stir up love before its time. You want to know when you know it is time? *When there is complete peace.* Do you have peace on all ends? Peace starts in your heart and mind. After that, those who love you will confirm the peaceful feeling you have inside. Peace is essential in your relationships.

What if I cannot wait to have sex; should I just get married? An old friend used to say to me, "Getting married to have sex is like buying a 747 airplane for the peanuts." My personal answer is NO! You can make it; just remember to have patience (another word for discipline) in your pursuit of love. It would be worse to be stuck in a marriage in which your only highlight is sex. This could lead to an array of disappointment and unmet expectations. Please don't make a poor choice on this one because the hotel will check you in automatically. If you choose well, healthy love will meet you on the narrow path of good timing.

Whew! Aren't you ready to put an end to this life-stealing action of lust? I certainly am, but it will come down to a daily decision of discipline in those four areas. You can do it!

––––––––––––

Q 3s

1) If sexual lust has plagued you, what are you going to do about it?

2) Name three people who you could keep in your life to help you avoid these problems. These are people you can talk to, ask questions of, and be real with.

3) Of the four disciplines, which one do you need to work on the most?

CHAPTER 5: **STUCK IN THE ROOM**

The world is full of suffering; it is also full of overcoming it. –Helen Keller

It was the brightest of summers, the most exciting of times. Love was in the air, baseball was on the ground, and your faithful author and friend had grown into full maturity. Yes, this was the summer going into the seventh grade. I was becoming my own man, making my own friends, and calling all the shots behind home plate as the self-proclaimed world's greatest catcher. I met a young lady working behind the concession stand; she used to give me free candy between innings. How could I not love her? She went straight for my stomach. Life was good. No, it was grand, until I slightly misspoke ...

As a young man, I felt as if I had all the answers and that my way was the only way. This led to an argument with my mom, and, of course, some major frustration on my part. So one thing led to another. My mom caught me on the phone, calling her a name that I cannot repeat in this book. See, not only am I a survivor of the Heartbreak Hotel, but also a survivor of the wrath of an out-of-control businesswoman from Philly. Hence the title of this chapter, "Stuck in the Room." You can imagine I did not leave my room for a long time after that. I was done for—not to mention that I had some major apologizing to do after calling my mom that name.

The point is that most of our frustrations are over stupid things. I am positive that my anger in this situation was not validated. I probably wanted to go somewhere or do something that no seventh grader had any business doing. Because I got told no, the child in me went on attack rather than just accepting it. It is funny looking back on the things we used to get mad at and realizing how little they actually matter. My entire life, all my mother ever wanted to do was protect me. She had no ulterior motive for punishing me. I wanted what I thought was more fun, more free time, more opportunity, and more people to play with. From my immature standpoint, I thought her saying no meant she was giving me less, when actually it preserved more for me later on in life. *We often think that when life gives us a no, it means never, or worse, it means less of all that this life is capable of providing. In actuality, "no" or "not now" can be our greatest source of heartbreak prevention.*

Remember in the first chapter I told you I stayed in a hotel at the beach? Well, there were several days my family would be stuck inside that hotel due to weather. Forget shark attacks; Florida's reputation for lightning strikes is much deadlier. It was not safe to go play in the water when it was storming. We understood the importance of safety precautions, because they make mistakes avoidable. Again, let me reiterate to you the importance of staying out of harm's way. It might sound like I am encouraging you to stay in your hotel room. Let me be clear: *I am not telling you to stay in any room at the Heartbreak Hotel*. But without the two uniquely designed safety barriers of maturity and authority (things my mom wanted me to respect), we humans are a hazard to ourselves. As we continue our discussion on lust, I am going to debunk the theory that more is better. *An individual who is content under authority is an individual well on his way to utmost maturity. It is only by maturity that we achieve sustainable promotion, eventually leading us to more than we could have ever asked for or imagined* (see Eph. 3:20). Your dreams and goals rest solely on the heels of contentment, of trust. It is difficult, though, for brokenhearted individuals to trust, and that is completely understandable. Even still, trust is the hand you hold when you are dangling off the edge of the cliff. Without the hand, you most certainly can fall, but with the hand, you might just live a life full of abundance and satisfaction. Yet, so many refuse to apply these protective virtues and they stay stuck in their hotel room. Just like disrespect grounded me, your lust for more paralyzes you.

More vs. Maturity

Like we talked about in Chapter Four, lust is costly. It is so costly that it can kill you. Beyond the fact that unhealthy and untimely sexuality is deathly; an unhealthy desire for more might even be worse. Hear me now: there is a fine line between desiring healthy success and becoming filthy greedy. Unfortunately, the original "American Dream" has been so distorted that we can barely see the proper intent of it even when we study it. Our founders ventured to these shores to establish a freedom to worship, a freedom from oppression, and an ability to build community around common values. The intent was never to build social clubs for churches, empower corrupted medias, celebrate lazy parents, or even scoff at personal responsibility. What have we become? Even worse, what will we become? This is a result of the disease I call *more*.

More drives us away from our original motives; it minimizes the importance of why we started in the first place. *More is actually less, not the other way around*. More money, more things, more position, more property, and more status only equates to more challenges, more pride, more stress, more self-reliance, and more strained relationships with the people who need more of you. Sometimes less income, fewer things, lower positions, not as much property, and smaller status equates to more financial freedom, more time with those you love, more opportunity to open your home, or even more flexibility to do the things you actually

73

enjoy. Now, some people are fantastic at balancing more because they have figured out the massive importance of maintaining their major priorities. I can bet that those individuals are saying no more than they are saying yes, and removing more than they are adding. Again, acquiring wealth or growing in status is not wrong in any way, shape, or form. In fact, it can even be a sign of God-promotion. What I am getting at is the motive of the heart—the *why* you want to be who you want to be. *Maturity always trumps more.* Maturity is the wellspring of maintaining peace with men and acquiring influence with people. As we discussed in Chapter Four, sexual lust is managed and defeated by discipline. The lust for more is managed and defeated with maturity. How's that for a one-two punch? Discipline and maturity are the thunder and lightning of heartbreak management and hotel evacuation.

Let's learn a bit about maturity from my friend Joseph. Joseph, who was known for his ability to interpret dreams, experienced a crazy childhood full of heartbreak and despair. He had every reason to grow up angry and bitter at the world; he had every reason to fail and use his childhood woes as an excuse. For some reason, though, he overcame a few things. He overcame the fact that his brothers planned to kill him but instead sold him into slavery. He overcame the fact that he was wrongfully accused and thrown into jail to die. He overcame time and time again, and with his overcoming, he became a standard for success.

Tumultuous experiences will either produce maturity and perspective, or they will check you in to the Heartbreak Hotel. Everything in life is a choice, oftentimes a choice of attitude and your willingness to be flexible. In this verse, Joseph chooses flexibility and maturity as he reveals his identity to his brothers for the first time in years, after they have sent him off into slavery.

> So it was God who sent me here, not you! And he is the one who made me an adviser to Pharaoh—the manager of his entire palace and the governor of all Egypt (Gen. 45:8).

Maturity allows us to lead who we are supposed to lead, submit where we are supposed to submit, accept our blessings when they come, love purely with proper motives, and live in utmost emotional health! Maturity will take us places we can never go ourselves. It gives us grace to forgive and move on to greater heights, from one glory to another, ultimately taking us from the hotel to our home.

As mentioned above, Joseph's brothers sold him into slavery; they did not care if he lived or died. They just wanted him out of their sight. He was a dreamer, a visionary, and his father loved him more than he loved the other brothers. None of those things were Joseph's fault, but he did get punished for it. At least, we would consider betrayal a form of punishment. Maybe for a time, Joseph held hurt in his heart; for a time, he might have even been bitter. But the Bible only highlights the grace and maturity in which he walked. It is so crazy that throughout all the highs and lows of his life, he succeeded. For instance, when Joseph was in jail, he was excellent. When he was a servant, he was great. Tell me how someone goes from being a slave to being a servant to being in jail to being a governor? It's simply called *maturity.* He was resilient in the fact that *his past was not going to determine his future.*

The craziest thing about this whole story is how his maturity saved and preserved generations. Egypt was in an economic recession and Joseph predicted it. He was in the wrong place at the right time. That wrong place was jail, and it turned out to be the right place for his God-given destiny. Because he interpreted a dream, predicting a famine (recession), his terrible and unjust circumstance provided an opportunity to voice his gift, which as a result promoted him and saved all of Egypt.

Let's look at Genesis 47:13–17:

Meanwhile, the famine became so severe that all the food was used up, and people were starving throughout the lands of Egypt and Canaan. By selling grain to the people, Joseph eventually collected all the money in Egypt and Canaan, and he put the money in Pharaoh's treasury. When the people of Egypt and Canaan ran out of money, all the Egyptians came to Joseph. "Our money is gone!" they cried. "But please give us food, or we will die before your very eyes!" Joseph replied, "Since your money is gone, bring me your livestock. I will give you food in exchange for your livestock." So they brought their livestock to Joseph in exchange for food. In exchange for their horses, flocks of sheep and goats, herds of cattle, and donkeys, Joseph provided them with food for another year.

Only maturity and desperation can take lemons and make lemonade. Doesn't that statement make sense in this scenario? It really was only through Joseph's confidence in his identity and his God-given gift set that he was able to have enough foresight to provide.

Unfortunately, maybe you are in your own jail; maybe your circumstance or situation has you down. Maybe you have held some bitterness or even envy toward others. *Today*, this must end. *Your circumstance is merely an opportunity to expose your gifts*, a chance for you to shine. *Darkness is the only place where light has a chance to be light. Face darkness, because there is a whole lot of light in you!* By the way, as you can tell from verse eight, Joseph got over what his brothers did to him. Maturity always recognizes there is a process in the plan; it knows that the painless road is not always God's road of great purposes.

Missing the Sunshine

Here's what we have not established about maturity: contentment is the seed that births it. Once contentment meets trials, it finally produces maturity. Contentment smiles at the trials and defeats its instability; this then lays the foundation for a life of balance and fruitfulness. If you make a choice to be at peace with who you are and content with what you have already been blessed with, you automatically have the will power and ability to conquer any trial or disappointment that life may bring your way.

I would like to close this chapter with one my favorite verses in the Bible. This verse provides me with the deepest challenge. Everyone talks about Philippians 4:13, which says, "For I can do everything through Christ, who gives me strength." This is a celebratory verse, easy to digest and easier to recite. Yet what comes before it is truly the prerequisite for moving mountains; it is the must have before we can go and do. Paul writes in Philippians 4:11–12,

> Not that I was ever in need, for I have learned how to be content with whatever I have. I know how to live on almost nothing or with everything. I have learned the secret of living in every situation, whether it is with a full stomach or empty, with plenty or little.

What a wild verse! I read that passage almost every day. The point is that *you are not actually missing out on anything if you don't have more of what does not last*. Cars will break down, homes will deteriorate, and even money will lose its power. What really matters on earth is building a solid kingdom inside the heart. Desire more love, more laughter, and more health. Live to bring more joy to others and watch it stitch up your once-broken heart.

We are halfway there! Don't give up yet; freedom is on the other side, waiting for us. I do have an inclination, though, that you are feeling a bit of freedom already.

————————

Q 3s

1) What is it that you lust for more of?

2) If you needed to remove one thing from your life, what would it be?

3) Who is one person that needs more of your time?

(PART 3 - HOUSEKEEPING)

CHAPTER 6: **THE MIRROR TEST**

Pain has a way of clipping our wings and keeping us from being able to fly ... and if left unresolved for very long, you can almost forget that you were ever created to fly in the first place. –Wm. Paul Young, The Shack

You have really made it far; let me reiterate how proud of you I am. This is really tough stuff, but you are a fighter! All of a sudden, we are here in Part Three of this book: *Housekeeping*. It is time to clean up that room, time to wash off all the mud you dragged in with your suitcase. Just like the first half of the book, we are going to have to talk in the form of truth. We have to go right to the source: our heart. I know you are ready ...

Transformed

A few years back, I was in Modesto, California, for a wedding. The night before the wedding, we groomsmen took the groom-to-be down to San Francisco for our bachelor celebration. I will never forget the drive into San Fran; driving in over the bridge that night was spectacular. Unfortunately, I was exhausted from trying to book a hotel room all day. Nothing was available on this Friday night except high-end, center-city towers. Trust me, I know, I called a hundred places. Now, fortunately for us, my salesman-like instincts took over. At barely nineteen years old, I hustled the fancy hotel for a cheaper rate, all this so that five dudes could crash downtown. I am pretty sure I got the concierge down an entire two hundred dollars. If I ended the chapter right here, this would be victory enough for me. Now that you know me, though, you know there is much more to discuss.

As we headed upstairs, I was reminded of our game plan for the evening. What you may or may not know about San Francisco is that it is known for all kinds of interesting things. One thing in particular is that men and women alike enjoy cross-dressing. We thought that if the groom dressed as the opposite sex, we would fit right in; we would put a sign on him and walk around town enjoying the evening. We must have fought with our groom for an hour about putting on the flashy outfit we purchased earlier in the day. Eventually, though, he tried it on—until he looked at himself in the mirror.

When our groom stood in front of the mirror, what he saw did not resemble anything that he was formerly. He walked into the hotel with street clothes. Now he was about to go downstairs with a skirt, makeup, some plastic jewelry, a halter-top, and a wig. We transformed him! Although very funny, this is exactly what happens when we stay inside the hotel: it transforms us into something we never intended to be.

Originally, our pain is internal; that is what checks us in. Eventually, our pain is so deep on the inside that we become numb to it. Before too long, the inside hurt translates outwardly, where everyone can see that something is wrong. Our groom was not about to let people see him looking like this! He had sense enough to know how crazy this was. On the flip side, those in the Heartbreak Hotel don't have that sense; they are blinded to it. Some even confuse their pain for style or self-expression. It is self-expression, all right. People are expressing their grief, hoping someone will take notice and attend to their suffering. What about you? Are you wearing an outfit of grief in the form of sorrow and pain? Once again, the formula for solving these problems is found inside the miracle of hope. Hope is going to help us pass this test, so come with me as I explain further ...

The Mirror Test

Sometimes when I am teaching, I will use a mirror and mud as an illustration to prove my point. What I like to do is have someone from the audience come up and look at himself in the mirror. Then I will have him throw wet mud on it and direct him to look again. Next, I ask the question, "Can you see yourself now?" The response is always the same: "kind of," "barely," or "no." Of course they can't see because there is mud where their face used to be. The mud is representative of the outfit; the mud is the craziness that we put on to cover our internal pain. It shifts the focus from the inside and redirects it to the outside. For some, it is as simple as more makeup. For others, it is as far as cross-dressing or putting fifty-eight colors in their hair. Now, let me make something very clear: I love style and abstract art; I completely dig fashion. There is a difference, though, between an individual who is naturally artistic and stylistic and an individual who is doing something to cover his insecurities. Let me take it further. So many of us put mud on our mirrors by lying to ourselves, convincing ourselves that we are something that we are not. This is not limited to just the things we wear or the makeup we put on. This could also mean our activities, social status, political stances, or even our spiritual misconceptions. The mirror test is simple: *When you look in the mirror, is it you that you see, or is it a faded, dirty picture of what was or what could have been?* That is a scary thought to dissect. So many of us start out with great dreams and even greater potential, but heartbreak, setbacks, and disappointment gets the best of us. *"What could have been" becomes the subtitle of our lives, resulting in a life wasted, not a life well spent.*

Who or what is it that you see when you look at yourself in the mirror? Is it heavy barbells on your shoulders? Is it black bags under your heart's eyes? Do you see cuts and bruises all over your metaphorical face? Can you even see your face? If you answer yes to some of these questions, there is a good chance you are a "preferred customer" at this hotel.

Thankfully, there is good news! The mud doesn't ever cover the entire mirror. For some, maybe it covers almost all of it. For others, maybe it covers half or a fourth of it. Even so, there is still a small resemblance of the original you. That you who had joy, hope, dreams, and promises is still somewhere behind the mud. Removing the mud, though, is tricky; it takes a cleaning magician, someone or something that can restore proper sight. There is hope for you yet, now to our formula for solving this problem ...

Fight Mud with Mud

Ever heard the phrase "fight fire with fire"? This is actually a real technique used by firemen. It started with early settlers, and they would deliberately raise small controllable fires, which they called backfires, to remove any flammable material in advance of a larger fire. They would do this so that they could deprive it of fuel. This literal "fighting fire with fire" technique was often successful and is still used today. *Sometimes, you have to use the enemy of your life to fight the enemy of your life.* This means confrontation is inevitable. *You have to be willing to confront what you fear with the same tenacity that fear confronts you.* This takes an extreme measure of courage, I do understand. Because you are desperate enough, pride is defeated, leaving you without any inhibitions. Finally, you will do whatever it takes to clean the mirror, whatever it takes to be free. Let me illustrate this firefighting concept more directly.

As Jesus was walking along, he saw a man who had been blind from birth. "Rabbi," his disciples asked him, "why was this man born blind? Was it because of his own sins or his parents' sins?" "It was not because of his sins or his parents' sins," Jesus answered. "This happened so the power of God could be seen in him. We must quickly carry out the tasks assigned us by the one who sent us. The night is coming, and then no one can work. But while I am here in the world, I am the light of the world." Then he spit on the ground, *made mud* with the saliva, and spread the mud over the blind man's eyes. He told him, "Go wash yourself in the pool of Siloam" (Siloam means "sent"). So the man went and washed and came back seeing (John 9:1-6) (Italics mine)!

I told you that you needed to fight mud with mud on this one. That is exactly what this mirror magician did. Jesus took the mud on this man's mirror (his blindness) and used it to make him see. I don't know where or when your pain started, but for this man, it started at birth. As soon as he was self-aware enough to know he was blind, he was discerning enough to know that something was wrong. What I find incredible about this story is the boldness of this blind man. It almost seems like he never gave up hope for seeing. He knew that vision was possible, so he kept his ears peeled in case one day his eyes might have the chance to open. The Bible does not say it, but you have to believe that he heard of Jesus. You have to believe that he listened to what Jesus said when he had this pre-healing conversation with him. *He used what was left to gain what had been missing.* Just like when you stand in front of the mud-filled mirror, you can still see a little bit of your own face. What hasn't been damaged within you? Dig deep and fight with it. That equates to the concept of seeing through the mud on the mirror. There is still a little bit of you that you can see; hold onto that hope and use it to your advantage.

Yet what is even more special was the urgency with which Jesus was willing to help the blind man. Christ had compassion, and the blind man must have felt it. At that point, he knew it was his chance, so it didn't matter to him what anyone thought. There was not a hint of pride from the blind man. I just wonder if you are fed up enough to not care who is listening or who knows how bad you have it. Once you get to that point, freedom is right around the corner. To me, it seems like Christ will take mud and transform it into healing water. This new water then allows you to finally see that original you, the person you were always meant to be. This is the muddy water he uses to clean off the mirror once and for all. This is God's concept of fighting mud with mud; this is how he exchanges your situation for his glory.

Who Were You Supposed to Be?

The scariest part about this chapter is what could happen if you stay dressed up, if you stay inside the hotel. You must—I repeat, you must—be willing to fight mud with mud. You were meant for something great. You were born to accomplish incredible things. Sadly, too many of us live in the hotel of what could have been. Here is what happens when you don't pass the mirror test:

My family's first home in Orlando was in a smaller subdivision, but families were quickly moving in. By the time I was in fifth grade, there were enough kids in the neighborhood to play full football games. There was even a field in the front of the neighborhood, which we made into a stadium of sorts. Most of my friends in this neighborhood were a bit older than I was. One in particular was much smarter than all of us too; his brother went to a major university in the state and had become a pharmacist. This friend of mine, who we will call Calvin, was on his way towards a similar destiny.

Calvin's family came from Europe, and I think most of his life, he felt disconnected from his folks. Communication was probably difficult at times; living in the shadow of his older brother could have even played a role in his gloom. I don't know exactly what it was, but Calvin began to develop some inner turmoil through high school, and it really came to a head when college began. By that point, most of the gang had moved out of the neighborhood and there was not a built-in group of close friends anymore. In time, Calvin's life began spinning. No, it was reeling out of control. He began to get involved in things like drugs, which moved him quickly into the lobby of the Heartbreak Hotel.

Eventually, Calvin met a young lady. He fell hard in love and they began to get serious, very quickly. For a while, I believe this helped some of his drug issues, but not for long. Time went on and Calvin's girlfriend found out she was pregnant. Because of this, she moved from Florida back to Georgia, where there was more family support. From what I understand about the situation, Calvin and his girlfriend were going through some major problems; the relationship was not headed in the right direction. So, he chased after her in attempts to soothe the relationship and take care of what he thought was going to be his child. *Here is where the story gets very difficult.* When Calvin got to Georgia, he found out the child was not his. Can you imagine how crushing that blow would be?

Calvin's girlfriend asked him to stay to raise the child, but even still, her concerns about his drug problem and how he would accept this news must have been high. Again, from what I know, Calvin agreed to raise the child. After all, he loved her and was in need of the purpose she provided. After hearing the news, Calvin explained he was going back to deal with a few things before he could relocate. When Calvin returned, he had a conversation with his father and told him that he needed one more night to soak the drugs into his system. He said he needed one more night to get out all his craziness, one more night to numb himself from reality. "Then, I'm getting my life straight. I'm checking in to a drug rehabilitation center first thing in the morning." This, of course, burdened his father, but because there was finally some hope for the situation, he agreed to leave Calvin alone.

All too often, we are willing to walk the tightrope of chance. That night, Calvin decided that he was going to take any and every drug he could get his hands on. It seemed like he was willing to take a serious chance with his life, regardless of the commitment to get it right in the morning. Sadly, Calvin was found face down on his pillow the next day, dead. With blood running down his nose, it was obvious that he had overdosed the night before. Heartbreak. Heartbreak. Heartbreak. I will never forget that unbelievable call I received. Apparently, there were police swarming his home, investigating for days. It seemed that Calvin was in deeper than any of us knew. See, *heartbreak for you does not mean it is only for you.* Whoever you are, if you are heartbroken, others will be too. *Someone else will always feel the ripple effect of your pain and the decisions you make based off of your pain.* That is why this story is so incredibly tragic. Beyond the fact that we lost a friend, we lost a young life. We potentially lost a healer; we may have lost the next great medical discovery or even a serious advancement in cures. What if Calvin would have been the one who figured out the formula for cancer treatment or even developed the cure for AIDS? What if Calvin created medicine that slowed down or eliminated Alzheimer's? What if? What if? What if? Unfortunately, we will never know ...

Look, I know the chances of his doing any of those things were slim to none, but the odds were stacked against most people who changed the world. You just need to be reminded how necessary it is that you pass this mirror test. *You have to ask yourself, as you are standing in front of that mud-covered mirror, not who could you have been but who can you still be?* That is the question for you right now or whenever you feel like you are faced with very dark circumstances. That question should plague you, terrorize you, drive you, push you, move you, stir you, wake you up at night, and cause you to believe in the impossible. More important, it should force you to pursue the impossible. Passing the mirror test goes way beyond your checking out of this hotel; it is all about you going and changing the world! What are you waiting for?

Q 3s

1) Is there mud on your mirror? If so, are you ready for it to be gone?

2) What is your greatest dream? What is your mission in life?

3) What mud miracle do you need to take place in your world, family, and self?

CHAPTER 7: **DO NOT DISTURB (THE RELATIONSHIP CHAPTER)**

Relationships are like glass. Sometimes it's better to leave them broken than try to hurt yourself putting it back together. -Author Unknown

As I was thinking about the title of this chapter, I was reminded of a story a buddy of mine told me. If this story is true, which he swears it is, then I am associated with sick people. Anyway, the story goes like this: it all started at a wedding. These two young bucks, full of a whole lot of zeal but less brain matter, made an incredibly ridiculous decision. They procured a key to the newly married couple's hotel room. From what I understand, the couple was staying in this hotel and leaving in the morning for the honeymoon. This is a normal occurrence, of course, but I guess one of these young fellers was in charge of prepping the room. Well, sure enough, they prepped the room. Apparently, they prepped the room so well that they hid under the bed the entire night! I will elaborate no further. God forgive them. I can't even imagine their exit strategy in the morning. How and what would compel these individuals to disturb and violate their dear friends on their first honeymoon night?

I can't lie to you; I am snickering as I write this. As sick as it is, you have to admit the humor in it. What is worse, this isn't the only story similar to this I have heard from my posse. Let me just say: on my wedding night, or anytime I am staying in a hotel, you best believe I am doing a room search. The "Do Not Disturb" sign is going up, immediately.

What is so crazy about this story is that this scenario is the ultimate "Do Not Disturb" moment. I mean, how often is it that we are on our honeymoon? We don't want any disruptions there. In fact, how often are we away on vacation? Again, that is the last place we want to be disturbed. I hate it when I am sleeping in a hotel room and I hear a loud, obnoxious knock on the door and it is the maids telling me they are there to clean. When I am in a hotel, I do not want to be disturbed! Unfortunately, though, this is a major problem in the Heartbreak Hotel. I would venture to say that you might be living in this hotel if you hate the idea of someone disturbing your relationships, or translated differently, knocking on the door of your heart. This is a huge sign, I mean, a massive sign that heartbreak is waiting to happen! This is more like an epidemic, a complete catastrophe on the horizon. Excuse me; I am about to cause you a disturbance you won't forget ...

Disturbance

Here is what happens: there are so many people who engage in friendships or romantic relationships, and they will not let others in to see if everything is okay, to check if everything is clean and healthy. Now, I am not suggesting you let people be nosy and offer up information that isn't necessary. Nobody needs to know if your boyfriend is a good kisser or if your girlfriend has bad breath. What I am suggesting is that you have someone older and someone your age keeping your heart in balance. *You need people who are willing to ask you tough questions—questions that help protect your present and preserve your future.* Your distance from safety is always self-imposed and isn't anyone else's fault but your own. Because this distance usually begins when improper action within the relationship starts, we are too embarrassed and prideful to talk about it. I do understand that some of us are not blessed with people in our lives who care like this. I am incredibly sorry for that. I wish I could be there for you. At the same time, you have to go find them. They do exist, and *your heart still must beat; therefore, it must be protected.*

At the root, the word disturbed means to interrupt. *Sometimes your greatest help can be the most obnoxious disturbance.* Some of you desperately need your relationships disrupted with accountability and boundaries. Without accountability and boundaries, your heart is subject to get dragged like a dog on a leash. Boundaries within our relationships act as a fence, protecting us from getting hit by a car while chasing a squirrel across the street. Yes, I just compared all of us to dogs. It is true, though; love frees us to run as hard and as fast as we want. Still, *love needs a fence of protection; otherwise we will get lost or run over.* With that said, please don't use boundaries as an excuse to keep your walls up. *Boundaries and accountability disturb your isolation and keep you protected.* It was your lack of boundaries that built the walls of this hotel in the first place. Accountability desires to take a sledgehammer to these walls and end your heartache for good.

This next chapter is going to deal with relationships from a romantic perspective. I am going to outline some relationship dos and don'ts. I am warning you: you will be disturbed and forced to make a choice between walls or boundaries. This chapter is applicable to anyone wanting to date or be married, especially for those who are dating currently. I would even bet this could help married folks as well. What you are about to read is general and practical application gained from conversations and failed experiences. A lot of these principles have been touched on already in this book, but they are more specific here so you can apply them to your relationships right now. I am confident that these principles will ring in your ears loud enough for you to hear the sound of freedom in both your good and bad relationships.

One more thing before we tackle what I have deemed as the "Definite D's of Dating." The most important factor in cultivating healthy relationships comes from Paul's second letter to Timothy, chapter two, and verse twenty-two:

> Run from anything that stimulates youthful lusts. Instead, pursue righteous living, faithfulness, love, and peace. Enjoy the companionship of those who call on the Lord with pure hearts.

This verse is full of dating advice, and it should be taken into consideration. I want you to focus on the end of this verse first, as it is the very foundation for the beginning of the verse. "Enjoy the companionship of those who call on the Lord with pure hearts." To me, this simply means that we should *NEVER* romantically involve ourselves with individuals who don't share our same values. If they don't share the same values, how could they be going in the same direction? *A positive and a negative charge will always result in a negative charge.* So be careful not to cultivate chemistry with individuals who you know will take your positive force for this world and turn it into a negative impact. Only two who agree can pursue righteous living, faithfulness, peace, and true love. Without this concept, lethal heartbreak is inevitable.

Now, with that said, you are ready for the Definite D's of Dating!

1) *It's always <u>dangerous</u> when you go hunting.*

A few years back, a vice president of the United States was on a hunting trip. These guys deserve a vacation once in a while, a time to blow off some stress. Except, on this trip, he accidentally shot his hunting partner. Yes—I repeat, he shot his partner with a gun. OUCH! I assume the V.P. was properly trained, but even those who are trained can fail in the things they do regularly. That is why it is so dangerous to go hunting for love. *I dare you to let love come to you in the form of patience and selflessness.* When you force things, oftentimes they just backfire. At some point, love will find you. You have to go about your daily life, but in doing so, pray that God develops your ability to love selflessly. Once he can trust you, it will be quite obvious as to who and when. You will have peace! Peace is the most important element in cultivating a relationship. *Until you have it, stay away from it.* While single, take advantage of the opportunity to train your own self for marriage. It is important to form excellent habits, now ... ask yourself, what kind of disciplines am I developing? Am I preparing myself for someone else? Put the love rifle down so you don't force the dating stuff; enjoy and embrace your preparation. It is vital.

I read a statistic once that only nine percent of women and two percent of men found relationships at a bar or club. They say that most statistics are made up, but I bet this one is closer to true than false. So, my suggestion is that you stop your search for satisfaction and love; you will never be able to satisfy yourself quite like God can. Again, I don't know where you stand on spirituality, but there is something about being content in your current state. For me, I cannot find peace and contentment unless there is peace between my creator and me. If I gear all my energy and emotion toward him, God will not only build the ability for me to love and serve my future partner, but he will also build a fortress of wisdom around my heart.

I dare you to seek God first. Watch how everything else follows after that (see Matt. 6:33). *Let God determine the time, place, and location for love in your life.*

2) *Begin to <u>deal</u> with your issues before you take on someone else's.*

There is a common misconception that someone you date is going to heal all your pain and stitch up all your open wounds. Quite the contrary; if you can't stand on your own two feet, you are setting yourself up for a big fall down. Instead of healing wounds, another's love will eventually feel like poison in your veins if and when that person leaves you. Because there are holes in your heart, you have no love to pour back into the other person. How can anyone stick around if they are constantly contributing to a person that is unable to give anything back?

Andy Stanley wrote an incredible book called *Choosing to Cheat.* I am going to use an example from the book but in slightly different context. Stanley illustrates the burden we cause when we hand someone our own burdens. The burdens, of course, are representative of the things we care about and are responsible for. These burdens can be both good and bad. The specific individual in the story leaves a big burden in someone's hands and pleads with him not to drop it. He then tells him he will be right back. All the while, this burden is getting heavier and harder to hold onto as the day goes on. Eventually, the other person drops the burden and it shatters everywhere. Upon return, the burden owner becomes frustrated and heartbroken. Bottom line, you cannot give your burdens to people who aren't strong enough to carry them. This works in the opposite situation as well. Be careful adding emotional and romantic relationships in your own life when you are not ready. Ask yourself; do I still have some big things left to deal with inside my own life? It's okay if you do, just deal with your own before you add pressure to someone else.

Whether you like it or not, emotionally connecting yourself to someone in a dating sense requires you to help carry his or her burdens.

3) <u>Destroy</u> *past relationships before developing new ones.*

My belief is that you are playing with fire when you choose to complicate your life with a love triangle. *You will eventually burn your new flame's heart, your old flame's heart, and, most important, your own.*

When we hurt other people, they are not the only ones affected; this is a two-way street. You are going to get hurt too. Anytime there is a battle, both the defeated and the victor will have casualties and become maimed in some way. Bottom line, both parties are mixing and matching blood. Now, add a third or fourth party. It is going to be a war inside your heart and mind. The player or the cheater is a self-protector, but true love is an all-protecting force. The day of the player is dead. Just look at the definition of true love:

It does not rejoice about injustice but rejoices whenever the truth wins out. Love never gives up, never loses faith, is always hopeful, and endures through every circumstance (1 Cor. 13:6–7).

Love is all about the truth. Anytime you maintain a love triangle, it is impossible for the truth to win. In attempting to protect yourself, you end up hurting everyone else. The truth will always set you free; it just might hurt for a while. Remember, if you can't tell the truth, you aren't really living in love.

4) <u>Describe</u> *your intentions.*

I have heard it said that you should *never tease the animals!* You have to give them their food or stay away, because they will destroy you when hungry enough. Such it is with relationships. Without clear communication about your status in the relationship, someone will often get confused and hurt. People have to know where they stand; they cannot be teased with hope (see Prov. 13:12). At some point, an attack or a retreat is inevitable. You will either be bruised from fighting with them or they will leave you alone.

In colonial times, the man used to write a letter of intent for the woman he wanted to court or date. It is clear we are no longer in that time. That's fine, but there should be a level of respect that comes with these kinds of commitments.

Guys must take the lead on this. You were created first, and woman came out of your own rib. If the relationship is healthy, she will be protected under your arm. She should never be behind you, beneath you, in front of you, or above you. This woman should fit right next to you. What I mean by this is that you must set the tone for the direction and vision of your relationship. Your leadership should come in the form of gentleness, protection, purity, respect, and equality. Both sides need to clearly communicate their expectations for one another. Once communication is established, safe barriers can be built.

5) <u>Define</u> *parameters in your own heart and mind*.

Let me share with you a powerful Scripture that might set the stage for your parameter building:

Don't worry about anything; instead, pray about everything. Tell God what you need, and thank him for all he has done. Then you will experience God's peace, which exceeds anything we can understand. His peace will guard your hearts and minds as you live in Christ Jesus. And now, dear brothers and sisters, one final thing. Fix your thoughts on what is true, and honorable, and right, and pure, and lovely, and admirable. Think about things that are excellent and worthy of praise (Phil. 4:6–8).

Build boundaries out of truth, honor, integrity, purity, love, and admiration. If you do this, you cannot lose. *Certainly, pain and disappointment will knock at your hearts door, but you will be protected from ever letting evil thoughts and actions own you.*

Need I say anymore on this subject? Well, other than showing you how to build parameters. These seven Definite D's are their own set of parameters. Specifically though, you can do a few more things ...

Here are some simple parameters of protection:

If the bathing suit touches it, you shouldn't.

No sleepovers with your girlfriend or boyfriend.

Date in groups or use double dating.

Date in public. Stay away from being home alone.

While dating, be in before midnight. Nothing good happens after midnight!

Keep your clothes on at all times!

Date someone you are friends with first. Common interests trump physical attraction.

Keep a select few informed of your relationship struggles, your highs and lows.

6) Don't *neglect your balance beam;* denial *is your measuring stick.*

We are back to that "Do Not Disturb" sign again. When you are losing friends, neglecting extracurricular activities, and hating everything that isn't your boyfriend or girlfriend, it is time to get out of that relationship. Relationships need to be balanced. If you are in denial about that, you are still stuck in the hotel.

Here is how you will be able to understand the difference between jealousy and love: *when those who love you are on board, stay on the ship. When those who love you are jumping ship, get a lifeboat.* In other words, if those who truly love and care about you are not *for* your relationship, more than likely it is not healthy for you. These individuals, whether they are parents, teachers, or close friends, are *normally* not in it to ruin your happiness. When they are fearful of your relationship, be brave enough to run into their arms, not the arms of the individual providing a health risk to your life.

7) <u>Dip</u> *when* <u>dumped</u>.

I will never forget the first two girlfriends I ever had—in sixth grade and then late in seventh grade. Yes, you could say I was moving fast in the world. People always like to make fun of relationships pre-driver's license. I literally rode my bike to my seventh grade girlfriend's house on the regular. Yeah, I guess you could call it puppy love. Maybe it was real love. I don't know if I would ride 3.2 miles on a bike now! Later on, these young ladies found other boys who were good for them. Unfortunately for me, they found them while they were going out with me. Can you believe that? Can you believe someone might cheat on me?

What I find interesting, especially as I write this book, is the fact that I haven't forgotten about it. Granted, it isn't something I think about daily, nor am I mad about it at all. In fact, I am a friend to those young ladies today. Even still, it can be the simplest things from our past that stunt our growth when we don't address them.

Where I am going with this is simply that *a lot of times relationships just run their course.* Believe it or not, that is okay. I believe I heard Tyler Perry share something about relationships where he compared people to tree anatomy. Some individuals are deep rooted, invested, and they will be there forever. Others are like branches. They will be there for a while, but when the ultra-violent storms come, they will break off. Finally, others are like leaves, where a simple breeze takes them away. They are there for a season and gone the next.

The problem is that we get hung up on these leaves that left us and we forget to nurture our roots and branches. It is probably because the leaves can be beautiful in the fall, and that beauty hides the branches, stumps, and roots that have been there forever. *We have to be okay with enjoying people while we have them and then be at peace when it is time for them to go.* Not everyone is a lifer and that is all right. Believe it or not, the same goes with our romantic relationships. Sometimes we meet and date people who we think might be there for a while, and the next thing we know, they are gone. Instead of obsessing over them and living with heartbreak, let's take it for what it was and learn from it. It isn't failure unless we deem it so. Even if we deem it failure, we should decide to fail forward, not backward. *Each individual, whether he or she is harmful or helpful, provides us an immeasurable education.* Let's commit to learning, not to regretting.

There is a reason I am harping on this so hard, and it is because too many of us chase down what was not meant for our lives long-term. I am not suggesting you purposely get into stupid relationships just for a learning experience, nor am I suggesting you not fight for love. Just, sometimes, you have to know when to let go.

If you are dumped, release yourself and stay away. If you do the dumping, do the same. The in-between stage is detrimental for all parties. Remember that *no one wins when nothing is defined.* Honestly, you better your chances of getting back together when you just let them miss you. Instead, we text and blow up their phone to the point where they won't ever miss us because we don't let them. Sometimes, people are overwhelmed by love and maybe they just need a moment to sit back and reflect. All of us deserve some space from time to time; all of us deserve a chance to do the right thing and make the right choice.

This is why I suggest you eliminate the term "friends with coupons" or "friends with benefits" from your vocabulary. You are much better than that; I really hope you know this to be true. In fact, when the Creator of the Universe formed you, he made no mistake. You were not designed for someone's sexual fix or booty call. Whether you believe it or not, this is the truth about you:

What marvelous love the Father has extended to us! Just look at it—we're called children of God! That's who we really are. But that's also why the world doesn't recognize us or take us seriously, because it has no idea who he is or what he's up to. But friends, that's exactly who we are: children of God. And that's only the beginning. Who knows how we'll end up! What we know is that when Christ is openly revealed, we'll see him—and in seeing him, become like him. All of us who look forward to his coming stay ready, with the glistening purity of Jesus' life as a model for our own (1 John 3:1–2, MSG).

If people want to let you go, just let them do it. They may not understand who you are. So don't play around with fire; don't give them their cake and let them eat it too. Here is your rule of thumb: they either commit to you or get none of you.

All Clean

There you have it: the seven Definite D's of Dating. How could you ever go wrong? Of course, we can all go wrong in a lot of ways. My hope is simply that you apply these truths and principles so that you can avoid unnecessary heartbreak and trauma. Oh, and now you have some accountability and boundaries too … No excuses anymore!

––––––––––––––

Q 3s

1) Is there a specific Definite out of the seven that you need the most help with?

2) Who is it that you might be able to keep in your life who would be willing to help you through your relationships?

3) What are you going to do now to avoid heartbreak in your romantic relationships?

(PART 4 - CHECKING OUT)

CHAPTER 8: **PACKING YOUR BAGS (THE FORGIVENESS CHAPTER)**

But pain insists upon being attended to. God whispers to us in our pleasures, speaks in our conscience, but shouts in our pains: it is his megaphone to rouse a deaf world. –C. S. Lewis

Welcome to the all-important final three chapters of this book. Truly, you are about to embark on the most important and significant stage of hotel checkout. Everything leading up to these three chapters has been incredibly important to your survival and will continue to be necessary for sustaining freedom. Still, without the execution of the next three phases, you won't check out or stay out of this hotel.

What is the game plan you ask? One word: *thrive.* Your choice to thrive outside the walls of this hotel is actually your only chance to survive. Please understand, when I say thrive, I mean that for your survival you must live a life that is exploding with purpose and promise. Once you leave, it won't ever be good enough to live with a mundane and apathetic attitude. You are about to become a great survivor! Survivors are normally the best storytellers, simply because they have been through things that have crowned them with credibility. Your time in this hotel is the greatest creative writing class you will ever be in. Your story is going to change the world and right now it is being written ... I hope that you will to commit to reading the next three chapters with an even more open heart and an even more open mind than the first seven. The remaining three chapters will ignite inside of you the lasting energy you need to live life outside the walls of the Heartbreak Hotel.

Now, before we go on, I must tell you one thing. I have included a small portion of my spiritual beliefs inside this handbook for heartbreak freedom. Maybe for some it has been more than a small dose. However, *the acquisition of your freedom will only happen through supernatural dependence.* The rest of this book will be unashamedly spiritual. It will be full of "Jesus this" and "the cross" that. What you are going to find out is that no matter what you have been through, or the questions life might bring tomorrow, the living story of the cross holds the answers to it all. *Independence is a result of complete dependence on the cross*, and it is only through the cross that hearts and minds might be opened. I sure hope you are willing to go another few rounds with me, because your checkout depends on it.

Running Out of Clothes

To me, there are few things more fun than traveling. At the same time, there are few things less fun than running out of clothes when traveling. Most hotels don't do your laundry for you or drop you off at the nearest Wal-Mart, which is why I cannot stand it when I run out of the essentials!

What about an airline, ever lost your luggage? Or have you spilled something on your valuable clothes and ruined them? I have been fortunate enough to avoid both of these outrageous incidences when traveling. Although, I have seen it happen to others and it makes them miserable. Sadly, life can often stain our clothing, lose our valuables, and remove our trust within society. Baggage is an essential item for any traveler, but getting attached to our luggage makes checkout near impossible. As you continue to read, you will find that the luggage has got to go!

Anyone who has ever checked into this hotel brought bags with them, but anyone who has ever checked out has left those same bags there. By the time you are ready to walk out those doors, you want nothing to do with the old, beat-up, stained clothes you once wore. Those are not the clothes of a conqueror; they are the clothes of a prisoner.

You, my friend, are not meant to be a prisoner; you were meant to be a victor! The hard part is that you have carried those bags with you for so long that they are almost a part of you, like your favorite pair of jeans or jewelry. You probably don't even know what it is like to live without them. Just like leaving a relationship that you have invested so much time in, walking away from your bags is just as hard, if not harder.

If you have been reading this book, chances are you know exactly what is in those bags of yours. So the question now becomes, "How do I detach myself from them?" It is good you asked! As I mentioned before, your independence from these bags happens when you finally get dependent on the cross. This cross I speak of is undoubtedly the cross of Christ. This cross obliterates the baggage; it dominates it by exemplifying one ultimate theme: *forgiveness*. It is only through forgiveness that you can embrace the full measure of the cross. I believe that this is why so many people reject the abundant blessing of salvation. So many people refuse to forgive others, refuse to forgive themselves, and then refuse to accept God's forgiveness. That's right, there are actually people who have held anger in their heart toward their maker. In fact, someone reading this book right now feels that deep within their soul; some even hate God.

Let me empathize with everyone for just a minute. There are a lot of people who have been through things that I could never write down in this book. Someone reading this has lost his mother to cancer and has never gotten over it. He has blamed God and others and has never been the leader, parent, or friend he was meant to be. Somebody else has done terrible things to those she loves. She has stolen or lied, abused or even tortured her own family, and has never been able to forgive herself for it. There are even individuals who were abandoned by their parents and have had to literally hustle on the street to find love, acceptance, and shelter. There is a world of kids with no dads, no love, and no hope. Now we are talking about justified anger, understandable pain, right? Well, yes and no. In the natural sense, it is completely acceptable for all of these individuals, including you, to wear this baggage, to settle in this pain, and never forgive. *But* why would we stay in the natural when the supernatural is available to all of us?

The cross is the supernatural element upon which we can solely lean. Everything that ever happened from the beginning of time, to everything that happens right now, is a reflection of the cross. *The whole point of our existence is to approach the cross just as we are; the whole power of the cross is receiving the forgiveness that changes who we will become.* It is even at the cross that all seen and unseen justice comes forth. Too many of us think justice should be served on earth, and though there is nothing wrong with trying for it, ultimately, it won't ever fully happen within our human existence. This is another key element in why so many of us are angry and disappointed.

For instance, most everyone is extremely disappointed in the ruling of a 2011 murder trial, in which the mom was accused of murdering her two-year-old daughter. If you do not know, she walked free because there was not enough evidence to convict her. The natural cry of all our hearts asks: where is the justice? My answer: it rests at the cross. Again, I am not suggesting we don't actively pursue justice; what I am saying is that when we don't get it in the natural, we leave it be at the only supernatural source. It is in the supernatural that we find peace in the most impossible and misunderstood circumstances; *only the supernatural empowers us to forgive.* Going forward, I will teach you how to receive forgiveness and give forgiveness through the only means possible: the supernatural cross.

Leave the Bags

September 11, 2001, was my sophomore year, and I was on the varsity football team. I will never forget that day as long as I live, but for more than just one reason. Besides being one of our nation's worst tragedies, 9/11 represents a unique moment for my personal life as well. This other significant benchmark is the day Jesus prompted me into serving in his ministry as a vocation. From that day on, I invited just about everyone in my school to my youth group, and almost everyone else I knew to church. Now, our youth group met on Wednesday nights, and I must say, we had a pretty awesome thing going—about a thousand students every week. We also had a halfway cool youth pastor who has found a way to stay halfway cool for almost twenty years. I wish I could show you some of the newspaper stories of my football team going to church together, or the pictures of my teammates with their jerseys on, hands held high to heaven. Those were incredible moments for me. I wouldn't take those back for ten lifetimes.

As my senior year of high school rolled around, like most seniors, I was struggling with what I was going to do after graduation. Where would I go? Would I play football in college? Would I move away and find a job? Would I stay and work at my church? I do think I got my answer on one particular night. During my senior year, I dated an incredible young lady who was a year older than me and in college at the time. Yes, I was dating a college chick in high school; you will remember me after this book! So, this young lady lived in a house near my high school with a few of her college friends. I asked them if I could use their house on Tuesday nights as a place for my friends to hang out and be together before we all would separate after graduation. They agreed and even made food for us.

One night, I told all of my friends who came on Tuesday evenings to meet me at the movies. I did not tell them what movie; I just told them a time and a place. Long story short, they guessed what movie we were going to see: *The Passion of the Christ,* as the film had just come out. Without any prior expectations, we all sat together and watched this riveting movie about the cross. *This evening changed my life.* It was in this moment that I knew what I was supposed to do and where I was supposed to do it. As soon as the movie ended, I stood on the chairs in the middle of the movie theater and explained to my friends that what they saw was real; the story of the cross was tangible for them, today. Collectively, they confessed their need for forgiveness, and we all prayed together in that theater for new life. Unfortunately, though, those kinds of prayers aren't magic. What so many people fail to realize is that *the cross is only supernatural for us when we choose to carry* it *rather than carry our bags.* So many of my friends and maybe even some of you have walked away from an encounter at the cross still wearing your stained and dirty clothes, simply because the exchange was too much to bear. You couldn't comprehend the thought of leaving your baggage with Jesus as he left his cross for you to carry.

Carrying the cross is the difficult part. When you carry it, you have to accept the fact that God actually does love you and wants to forgive you. Carrying it also forces you to forgive those who have painfully violated you. For your benefit, it does not expect you to maintain or cultivate relationships with those who have burdened and pained you. At the same time, it does require you to forgive them and let it go. What is so moving about the cross is that most of the time, something in you wants to bring peace and order to those broken relationships anyway. Once you have experienced forgiveness, you cannot ever live without it. *That is why carrying the cross is both the heaviest burden and the lightest load. The cross exemplifies beauty and blood, love and war.* At the cross, the blood of Jesus was shed so that the war for your heart could be won. The beauty of Jesus is found in his willingness to die for a very undeserving people. We are the undeserving people and our bags are full of garbage that makes us that way. Fortunately for us, the blood at the cross offers us the option to be cleansed completely; we just have to do our part. Your bags for his cross, will you make the exchange?

Your Bags Fly Free

A dear friend of mine, who is a captain for Southwest Airlines, constantly brags that he works for the greatest airline in the world. Maybe he is right; apparently, bags still fly free at Southwest. From a spiritual perspective, yours can too. Because *though it cost you everything to carry the cross, it costs you nothing to leave your bags behind.* Throw your baggage as hard as you possibly can at the cross; throw it as high as you can and watch the pain *begin* to fly away. Galatians 5:1 says,

> So Christ has truly set us free. Now make sure that you stay free, and don't get tied up again in slavery to the law.

My friends, these bags are slavery. We can chuck them and let them fly far away from our hearts and our lives. It is for our freedom that Christ will do whatever it takes to set us free. We have a golden opportunity to finally run without hundreds of pounds on our minds, bodies, hearts, and even churches.

In fact, according to all four Gospels, the Roman guards put a crown of very sharp thorns on the head of Jesus. This crown dug deep into his head, causing bleeding and probably a massive headache. To the guards, these thorns represented a king's earthly crown. As Christ claimed to be the Son of God, the Savior and King, they mocked him by putting it on his head. These sarcastic guards called him, "King of the Jews," and they began to make fun of him, spit on him, and even hit him with their fists and staffs. What I find so interesting is that Christ was simply on his journey towards his destiny. His destiny was to come and redeem the world, it was to seek and save whatever was lost, broken, and hurting. Sometimes, though, as we are approaching our purposes and destinies, people mock us, make fun of us, and bring added pressure and pain to our lives. Unfortunately, because of that, we give up on the journey, checking into the hotel instead of helping others checkout. Not Christ. He stayed the course and he stayed on task. He had to wear that crown because when the blood flowed from his head, it represented an exchange and transfer to our head and mind. If we want, we can leave our bags for the actual mind of Christ. We can leave our bags for higher thoughts, holy hope, and limitless vision. Yes, the mind of Christ allows us to dream bigger and greater, deeper and wider. The mind of Christ defeats disorders and destroys death. The mind of Christ enhances creativity and directs focus. It will take a culture of negativity and turn it into an army of positive power. The mind of Christ has taken a distracted boy with an attention disorder like me and allowed him to somehow pen this book. The cross is supernatural!

I must keep going, because your ability to walk free in forgiveness needs all four stages of the cross to be complete. With one down, we look at his body, which was tortured through men, by us. Yes, I said by us. The week before the crucifixion, Jesus rode into town on a donkey as the crowd sang "Hosanna," asking this same Jesus to save them. Which is exactly what he plans to do. Ironically, the same people who a week before asked for his salvation asked for his destruction. Sadly, we are doing the same thing today with our policies, our churches, and schools. We worship God on our money, but kill him by acting inappropriately within our government. We sing his praises at our sporting events, but we don't acknowledge his hope in our high schools. We even protect destructive religions, but shun the name of Jesus and actually run from the power of the cross.

This is not new news. It is simply the reality of the missing element in our nation, the reason we are broken. Thankfully though, as Isaiah 53:4–5 says, he was broken so that we might be whole again!

> Surely he took up our pain and bore our suffering, yet we considered him punished by God, stricken by him, and afflicted. But he was pierced for our transgressions, he was crushed for our iniquities; the punishment that brought us peace was on him, and by his wounds we are healed.

You get it now? They beat his body into complete submission. In his willingness to submit to this worldly authority, he attained all power, dominion, and authority in the universe over sickness, pain, disappointment, and even heartbreak. The Bible says that Jesus went to hell to take back the keys. For us, that means he is the key to getting out of this hotel. He is the key for healing from disease, promiscuity, insecurity, and lust. If you let him, he will once again make you a new creation. His bloodied body crushes drug addiction, alcohol abuse, sexual immorality, and all sickness. He is the rock, the key, the healer, the redeemer, the hope, and the plan. He is the king of freedom, and it rests at the cross, from the inside to the outside of his "broken" body. Once again, it is only attainable if we accept this forgiveness, only attainable if we exchange our bags.

Not only did they put thorns on his head, which transforms our minds, but they also annihilated his body, which heals our spiritual, emotional, and physical diseases. Can you believe there is more? Additionally, they pierced his hands and his feet with nails. This was their human solution for holding him to the cross. Fortunately for us, Christ was one hundred percent human and one hundred percent God. In this situation, though, it wasn't the human element that held him to the cross; it was the supernatural God element holding him. That supernatural God element can be defined by only one word: *love*. The pierced hands and feet of Jesus represent the kingdom of love he has built for all of us to live in.

Every time Jesus touched someone or something, it was delivered with supreme love. Everywhere he went, he walked in the complete fullness of love. We have gone a lot of places and done a lot of things. Some of us have built our own kingdoms of pain, brokenness, and disaster. In fact, some of us have built things that look like ministries but are really just self-absorbed monuments. Some have even done drugs with our hands; destroyed people and things with our hands; stolen with our hands; overeaten with our hands; murdered, molested, and made dirty money with our hands. At this point, you are beginning to understand that it is only by the supernatural cross that what you did yesterday with your hands is not what you will do today or tomorrow. His pierced hands provide you an opportunity to build a family in exchange, to build the church, to build the community, to build others, and even build yourself properly. Your hands, if you let them, can become his hands. You can begin to heal, you can raise the dead to life, you can mend hearts, and you can actually love. What will you do with the hands that God gave you?

In the same context, and as mentioned before, some of us have been to a lot of places that Jesus' feet never went. I do not mean this geographically, either. Some of us have lived our lives in nasty clubs, strip joints, alleys, and jail cells. We have walked a fine line between detrimental behavior and a destiny for death. Once again, transformation and exchange is even offered for where you will go tomorrow. It does not matter where you were yesterday or earlier today. What matters is that your feet take you to a better place tomorrow. Blessed are the feet of those who bring good news (see Rom. 10:15)! So go from here, walk in your promise of destiny. Bring good news and hope wherever you go, to whomever your destiny brings you to. If willing, your feet can now be his feet—fully blessed, fully capable, and full of real love. The world, your city, and this nation are yours for the taking, if you only walk in love.

Finally, according to the Word of God, when Christ died, something even more supernatural took place.

> Then Jesus shouted out again, and he released his spirit. At that moment the curtain in the sanctuary of the Temple was torn in two, from top to bottom. The earth shook, rocks split apart, and tombs opened. The bodies of many godly men and women who had died were raised from the dead (Matt. 27:50–52).

Incredible! This is so mind-boggling to me because this moment signifies the opportunity for the New Testament Church to start. Sure, Jesus raised up twelve men and a bunch of other people during his three official years of ministry, but those were just training and vision meetings. It wasn't until Jesus died that life could finally be injected into the veins of the church. What you have to understand is that the temple had a curtain and only the holiest of holy people, only the high priest could go in and represent you and me. As soon as

Christ died, we were all crowned priests; we were all qualified to go directly to our creator.

The fourth piece of freedom one must accept is to be free in the temple. Meaning, we are free to personally experience God in private and in public. The local church or the global church, when it is willing, has all the supernatural power it wants. It has the power to end poverty, to provide healthcare, to dictate culture, to create and enhance the world. It has the power to heal, to light, to hold, to protect, and even to fight. The church is you and I; the church is us! We have the power to force heaven to come to earth if we leave our old selves at the foot of the cross and hang our new selves on the cross. We have a choice to not only carry it, but also wear it.

Death is completely necessary for life. Forgiveness is ultimately a death to our pride and a death to our ambition. Without death, we cannot forgive, and without forgiveness, we cannot embrace the supernatural miracle of the everlasting love of Christ. That is all the cross is about, *death*. Christ died and now we must follow his lead, so that we can be resurrected out of the hotel into something more beautiful and significant.

The Daily Funeral

Jesus is coming back and the Bible is clear that he does not start works that he doesn't intend on finishing. You are his greatest work and he will finish you to perfect completion if you let him.

You can be clay in the hands of a master potter, and he can mold you into a perfected shape, a beautiful decoration of grace. That is what he is coming back for: a reconstructed individual, willing to receive his life-altering renovation. Attain this revelation and you will be on your way to complete redemption from anything this hotel has stolen from you.

As I close this chapter on the power of forgiveness, I have to teach you the final step. There was your head, exchanged for his mind. There was also the body exchanged for your deliverance, the nails for your building of love, and of course the freedom we now have in the temple. Finally, you must embrace the grave. *The grave is the gateway to resurrection.* If you refuse the grave, you won't experience resurrection in your own life. In a sense, Christ committed a holy suicide. He chose to die for our sins and burdens. This is one of those rare occasions in the history of the world that suicide was justified. He even said that there is no greater love on the planet than to lay down your life for your friends; and this is exactly what he did (see John 15:13). The reason is simply because he knew that without death, there can be no resurrection. The cross is pointless without the resurrection; death is hopeless without the opportunity for others to live. So as we close, here is your call to die so that you might just live, so that Christ can resurrect beautiful life through you.

> He must become greater and greater, and I must become less and less (John 3:30).

> Not everyone who calls out to me, 'Lord! Lord!' will enter the Kingdom of Heaven. Only those who actually do the will of my Father in heaven will enter. On judgment day many will say to me, 'Lord! Lord! We prophesied in your name and cast out demons in your name and performed many miracles in your name.' But I will reply, 'I never knew you. Get away from me, you who break God's laws' (Matt. 7:22–23).

To me, these are two of the scariest Scriptures in the Bible. Literally, *we cannot live with these Scriptures and we cannot live without them.* Let me explain.

Paul speaks to us through Philippians 1:21 and says, "For to me, living means living for Christ, and dying is even better."

Now, Paul is speaking about a physical life and death. If he dies, he is with Christ; if he stays alive, he gets to live for Christ. He goes on to explain that he will be more fruitful for Christ alive. Even still, Paul understands that truly living for Christ means dying. *The reason Paul speaks so freely and comfortably about death is because he is already dead.* Paul is dead to his flesh, his selfishness, his will, his desires, his hopes, his dreams, his needs, his ambitions ... For Paul, it was never about the miracles or the moments; it was only ever about the mission.

Really, to fulfill the Scriptures above, you must commit flesh suicide. *The more dead you are to you, the more alive Christ is within you.* Hence, he finally becomes greater and you become less. Once he is positioned at a greater place than you, you are capable of doing the will of God.

Oh, and by the way, if you are willing to let go of your own control and your own plans, then he is willing to let go of his perfect will and perfect plans for you. Meaning, *the things you desire will transform from forced success to perfectly timed God-promotion.*

This is my daily funeral. It can be yours too. Forgive and be free. Forgive and checkout of this dark and dreary hotel. Right now, I am praying for and believing in you with all my heart. This goes for every man, woman, and child. You don't even have to wait. Now is the time. Today is the day for your salvation. I implore you to run to the cross, to loudly call on Jesus! He is the only reason to live—I mean, the best way to die …

———————

Q 3s

1) Do you have a personal relationship with Jesus Christ?

2) Why is it so hard to leave the bags at the cross?

3) Will you accept the call of the cross? If so, say this prayer: Dear Jesus, I bow my head at the cross. You are all I've ever needed, and you are the reason I live. Wash away my sin, my shame, my heartbreak, and my pride. I confess that you are Lord! Come into my heart and my life. Transform me! Be the Lord of my life; be the complete master of it all. Amen.

If you prayed that, do four things. 1) Get a Bible. 2) Tell someone immediately. 3) Attend a "healthy" church that teaches the Bible. 4) Get baptized in water.

CHAPTER 9: **PAY THE BILL**

The only way to deal with an un-free world is to become so absolutely free that your very existence is an act of rebellion. –Albert Camus

For years, my mom has worked in the linen industry and dealt directly with hotels. Sheets and towels, pillows and comforters have been our lives for decades. When it comes to blankets or covers, I have never lacked. Sounds exciting, doesn't it? I think my mom has given more linen away than your local homeless shelter. In fact, she *is* Orlando's homeless shelter! I grew up in a giving home; it was the culture of our house and our business. I believe with all my heart that this is the stem of *all* our blessings …

According to my mom, as she was growing up, the law in her house was that if someone needed a place to eat or sleep, she was always allowed to bring that person home with her. When my grandmother tells her stories, she always claims that we need to help everyone, because anyone in need might just be Jesus. This always tickled my grandfather. Whenever he would answer a knock on the door of someone in need, his response was a holler back to my grandmother that "Jesus Christ is here again!" You have to laugh at that one ...

While staying here, we have accrued an additional debt by ordering room service and exploring all those extra amenities the hotel may have offered. Not to mention, some have been living here for years. That is a pricey bill, one that the richest of rich may not even be able to pay. Yet once again, the hero of humanity makes himself available to us at no extra cost. *Christ is here again* and is willing to swipe his debit card of grace for *all* who are wasting away in this run-down hellhole of a hotel. According to Romans, *all* have sinned and missed the mark. Let me show you:

> But now God has shown us a way to be made right with him without keeping the requirements of the law, as was promised in the writings of Moses and the prophets long ago. We are made right with God by placing our faith in Jesus Christ. And this is true for everyone who believes, no matter who we are. For everyone has sinned; we all fall short of God's glorious standard. Yet God, with undeserved kindness,

declares that we are righteous. He did this through Christ Jesus when he freed us from the penalty for our sins. For God presented Jesus as the sacrifice for sin. People are made right with God when they believe that Jesus sacrificed his life, shedding his blood. This sacrifice shows that God was being fair when he held back and did not punish those who sinned in times past, for he was looking ahead and including them in what he would do in this present time. God did this to demonstrate his righteousness, for he himself is fair and just, and he declares sinners to be right in his sight when they believe in Jesus (Rom. 3:21–25).

I cite these verses to reiterate my point that the price has been paid in full. You can be one hundred percent free, no questions asked and no strings attached. Just like with my grandmother and my mom, Christ is here, you just have to open the door of your heart and exit the hotel with him. He is the home for the homeless, the food for the hungry, the water for the thirsty, and the love for the lonely. This is the Christ that is both knocking at the door of your heart and waiting in the lobby of this hotel. When will you walk away from your circumstance and meet him? When will you choose to partner with King Jesus? He is the one and only way home.

Part of Departure is

Solidifying Your Partner

In the paragraph above, notice the word I use in reference to the king: *partner*. I am not referencing your mate but rather your partner who is paying your debt to get you out of this hotel. *The reason for checkout is not just for your freedom, it is also for the freedom of others.* Praise God for your healing, praise God for your freedom, praise God for your departure! At the same time, there is still a messy world that needs the same healing and deliverance that you are getting. You, my friend, are their answer; you are the hope of the nations. God does not pay your bill so that you can leave the hotel the same. God does not pay your bill so that you can go home with nothing to do. There is a responsibility to hotel checkout! Christ inside of you is the hope of the world, the hope of any glorious victory in your life (see Col. 1:27)! God is not only a giver of freedom but of responsibility too, because *freedom is never sustainable without a willing person responsible enough to maintain it.*

God the Giver

How then do we move forward and apply what I am talking about? What you have to understand is that *generosity is the key we use to start the engine of prosperous living.* Prosperity within our culture only happens outside of the hotel and can be initiated by a partnership with God. Post-hotel, it is our responsibility to become catalysts in bringing about true hope in the world. Of course, we do this by our generosity. Not only did Christ first love us, but through his love, he is generous to us, prompting us to show generosity and compassion to others. *Generosity eliminates years of regret by redirecting our focus to the now, not the then.* Please note, *generosity doesn't pay back, it pays forward.* That is why *true generosity looks for investments, not reparations.* Generosity refuses to handicap; it hopes to build bridges and repair broken wings. Once you have been given freedom, it is only natural to give it to others.

Since the beginning of time, God has been investing in your future. He knew you would be in this predicament, he knew you would need this bailout. That is why he sent his only Son into the world—not to condemn you but to save you from your living hell and ultimately from an eternal hell (see John 3:17). His investment of love holds no records of wrongs, and he exiles your former shame as far as the east is to the west (see Ps. 103:12). I believe that it is his generous nature that forces him to forget about your past and bless you in your future. Great investors and successful businessmen don't worry about what was lost; they go with what they have now. These people are crafty enough to work with what they have so they can build an enterprise of success and wealth later. It is now your responsibility to invest in tomorrow's successes. This mindset will usher you from your room to the lobby, where the Son is waiting to escort you home.

God the User (of Your Generosity)

Do you remember the story of David and Goliath in the Bible? Of course you do: the greatest underdog story of all time! This story is the original "American Dream." You know, rags to riches, look at him now! The shepherd boy knocked out the giant and eventually became a king ...

Okay, so this isn't just an American thing; this is originally a God thing. This is God's specialty. He takes individuals who are hidden away, unusable, and quieted, and then turns them into planet-shakers. David went on to become arguably the greatest king in the entire history of the world, with the exception of our King Jesus. For you, the same is true. *God isn't just paying your way out of the hotel; he is paying your way to opportunity.* This is the bill of the cross! It seems like the worse off you are, the more likely God is to use you. *Your potential significance isn't tied to your situation; it is tied to your willingness!* David wasn't the first pick of any man, but he was willing, so God blessed him. I bet a few of you haven't felt like anyone's first, second, or third pick. Don't worry about it! Trust me, if you are willing, God is willing to use and bless you.

One of my favorite verses in the Bible is found in Mark's rendering of the Gospel. The background of the story is very simple: a woman who had a very expensive jar of perfume decided to break it and wash Jesus' feet with it. According to everyone in the house, the perfume was worth at least a year's

137

pay. I'm not sure about you, but I wouldn't spend that much to wash the Queen of England's feet! Nonetheless, this woman knew Jesus was getting ready to pay a massive price for her freedom, so she wanted to partner with him. She wanted to prepare him for the cross, and more important, for burial. In those times, they had to prepare bodies for the grave so the smell of death would not be unbearable. This is exactly what she does here. And because of this, Jesus says,

> I tell you the truth, wherever the Good News is preached throughout the world, this woman's deed will be remembered and discussed (Mark 14:9).

If an unknown and formerly insignificant individual can impact the world by partnering with Christ, certainly someone like you has the potential to do the same through your willingness to simply be generous.

Build Your Own

Two generations have come before me and have invested into the art of giving. Whether you believe it or not, I could easily live off the harvest that these two generations have sowed. This does not sit well with me; I will disappear without work and lose interest without purpose. Unless I earn and toil for some of my own success, my belief is that I should not eat in abundance or dress in style. *A commitment to generosity dissipates laziness, enhances creativity, cultivates purpose, and ignites movement.* It is important to understand that *it isn't fair to only live off the blessings of the generation that came before us.* With a heavy heart, I believe that the majority of my generation is doing this. A lot of our forefathers toiled in fields for years and we have just reaped their harvest. Now that we live in trying times, some of those fields have been burnt and most of my generation does not know how to work hard enough to re-soil the ground. Hence the reason so many of us are stuck in this hotel, we are too emotionally and spiritually lazy to get out.

What if we gave like we were rich and spent like we were poor? That would help us earn our keep on the earth, but we cannot do this while sitting in the hotel. Success is restricted when you are cramped up and paralyzed. See, *some were born into success, others were groomed for it, but the most fulfilled individuals have spent their days grinding for their own.* In regards to hotel residents, we must begin the grind on out of here. *Do not let the regret of what you should have done keep you from what you should do now.* Sure, Jesus will check you out, but your commitment to him will keep you out.

Solomon, who was the son of King David, also catches my eye. He had several interesting conversations with God that inspired me to leave the hotel. Our former King David was a fantastic king, but throughout his life, he kept checking back in to the hotel. He had high moments, but low moments too. He murdered, committed adultery, and even lied. Because of this, he was not going to be able to build the dream in his heart. David dreamed of building a place for God, a house of worship if you will.

What I love about Solomon though, is that he knew it was necessary to build his own legacy, to add to the world with his own generous contribution. According to 1 Kings 6:11–14, and I am using my own paraphrasing, God said,

> Live the way I've set for you, do what I tell you, and I will complete the promise I made to your father; I will be with your people.

In other words, partnerships have both requirements and benefits. God showed Solomon that partnership with him brings about promotion. So that is what Solomon did (for most of his life). Not only did he build God's house; he also became the most powerful man in the world, as well as the wealthiest and wisest of all time. The benefits of partnering with God go way beyond your protection from the hotel; they incorporate God's original intention of hope and promise for your future (see Jer. 29:11).

I think by now you are grasping the concept of this chapter. As soon as you are ready, Jesus is waiting in the lobby, ready to pay your way. *The point, though, isn't about leaving; it's about what you will do when you leave.* What I am teaching you is how to stay out of the hotel. The best way to do this is to build a life of generosity and the greatest level of generosity is building his church with compassion. An even more specific way is to tell your story, help the needy, love the broken, and lead the lost home. You can also volunteer your time, give of your finances, and exude love through your words.

Walking with Christ compels you to donate generously to the world, and with that, you are protected from selfishness and pride. Yes I said pride—the reason that some of you stay in your room, or keep away from the altar. It is the reason you won't leave your bags, why you hold onto regret, and why you will stay in misery forever. *Kill your pride with generosity so that your heart might be built up with hope for humanity.*

Regret Retired

I will never forget meeting my friend Paul. While living in Orlando, I was playing flag football in a league with a bunch of my friends, and Paul was just hanging around the field. He was loud, boisterous, skinny, and talked like a New Yorker. Everyone seemed to know him except me, but he kept begging me to come into the game. I felt bad for the kid, so I told him if he had cleats by next week, he could play with us. Sure enough, Paul was there for warm-ups the next week, and he was holding his brand-new cleats. What was I going to do? So, Paul strapped his new shoes on and came into the game. He was even more loud and boisterous, but not very good at all. It didn't matter, though; we had so much fun watching Paul have fun that even though we lost, we were satisfied.

Later that night, I invited Paul to church and told him we played basketball once a week. Sure enough, Paul showed up with his basketball shoes and was even worse at this sport! As Paul got more involved and started coming around regularly, I began to notice that he was wearing some of the same clothes, riding his bike, and smelling more like the basketball court than a laundry room. Time went on and I found out that Paul had been living in the bathroom at the gas station he worked at. He was never able to shower, and he worked every day through the night. My heart went out to him. Eventually, we helped find him a place to live, and we constantly provided him with, you guessed it, linens!

Eventually, Paul had to move back to New York because there was not any more work for him in Florida. A few months went by, and one evening in the fall, I received a call from Paul. It was a delight to hear from him until he dropped the news that he was coming to Florida for Christmas and needed a place to stay. I encouraged him to not come; too many people were going to be out of town. That was the last I heard from Paul, until Christmas Eve, of course. As we walked up to the church, Paul was standing in the doorway, wearing a red shirt and wishing everyone the merriest Christmas of all time. I was shocked, of course, and even annoyed. I was annoyed because I told him not to come; there wasn't a place for him to stay.

After service, I frantically searched for a place for Paul to sleep. Somehow, this became my responsibility. No homeless shelters had space, no one else felt connected enough to take him, and most of my close friends were already out of town. So, reluctantly, I made the decision to take Paul home with me. I sound pretty selfish right now, don't I?

So, there we were, Christmas Eve, with dirty Paul and my parents. It was about two or three in the morning and Paul finally went to sleep. My parents and I traditionally open our gifts on Christmas Eve, and we found ourselves huddled in my parents' bedroom, frantically opening our gifts now that Paul was sleeping. Suddenly, though, it hit us as we were opening up our new phones and gadgets—what in the world is wrong with us? My mother even made the statement that this was not how she was raised! This young man had no one and came into our home and our world in need of love. We didn't know what his situation was in New York, what his childhood was like, or what was missing inside of him. All we knew was that Paul found hope in our church family, so he came back at what some consider the most depressing time of the year.

Immediately, a huge lump formed in my throat as regret began to control every paper I unraveled. I just couldn't take it anymore. Before we could finish opening our gifts, we hopped in the car and went to the only place that was open at two in the morning. We bought nearly everything we saw in the convenience store that night, including a stocking larger than three of Shaq's shoes put together. With every ounce of selflessness, we began to fill that stocking with candy, dollars, clothes, razors, and *linen!* We suddenly went from exclusive to as inclusive as we could possibly be. By the time the morning came, we were more excited about Paul opening his stocking than he was.

Later on, I found out that Paul's parents just didn't care what Paul was doing. Paul never had the educational opportunities, the social opportunities, or even the spiritual opportunities that the majority of young people in America have. Thankfully, the local church and everyday individuals were willing to come and rescue a potentially heartbroken young man. We will never know the full extent of what our compassion has done for Paul, but it doesn't matter. *Our generosity simply kept us from filling our own hearts with unnecessary things. While our hands filled a stocking with necessities, our generosity in turn filled our hearts with pure love.* As C. S. Lewis writes in *Mere Christianity,* "Love is the great conqueror of lust." Our lust of selfishness was broken by love. For that, I am grateful.

To this day, Paul and I communicate and even see each other from time to time. Our generosity has built a bridge into his heart forever. Paul continues to hustle his way through life, but he knows that the hotel isn't for him and it never has to be again. That alone keeps me focused on the goal, on the prize. Because partnering with Christ is the greatest journey one could ever take. When he pays the bill for us to leave, it is like he pays so much extra that we end up getting paid too. We get paid with purpose and then we pay his generosity forward. This is the essence of freedom; this is how your bill gets paid. Regret from the past is removed; it is overridden through generosity. Retire your regret today; take a walk downstairs and let Jesus pay your bill.

––––––––––––

Q 3s

1) What is keeping you from walking downstairs?

2) In what specific way can you become generous?

3) Do you have a Paul in your life and, if so, how can you help him?

CHAPTER 10: **GOING SHOPPING (THE HOLY SPIRIT CHAPTER)**

You cannot escape the responsibility of tomorrow

by evading it today. –Abraham Lincoln

If you read Chapter Nine, you can begin to tell that Part Four of this book is all about living outside of the hotel. Checkout is strictly preparation for successful life outside. Since you already left your bags and old clothes at the cross, it is time we go to the mall and pick out some new items. Obviously, I don't mean that literally, although, for some of you, it might be a good idea. What I mean is that when you have been given a new body, the old clothes don't fit anymore. There are those of you headed in a completely different direction; therefore you need new shoes for the journey you are now embarking upon. It is time to go shopping, time to put on a new armor of protection!

What Do I Do?

The story I am about to tell you, I left purposely for the end. This is probably because more than any of the other stories, this story launched the initial Heartbreak Hotel concept.

When I was a youth pastor in Dallas, I sat and counseled a lot of students and young adults. A lot of it was pretty basic stuff. "What do I do after high school?" "How do I know God is speaking to me?" Other times it would be a bit more serious. "My step-dad hits my mom." "My uncle molested me when I was younger." "I can't stop smoking weed."

Then one afternoon, one of those conversations that change your life walked into my office. A young lady who had been coming to our student ministry off and on for a couple of months said she really needed to talk. I could tell by having one conversation with her, there were some things that just weren't right. Insecurity was written all over her face, the way she stood, and even the way she walked. This was a battered young lady, broken and completely checked in at our old hotel. Whenever I counseled students, especially girls, I always kept a female leader in the room with me for my protection. One lie can ruin a young man's life, and I was not about to let that happen. This day was no different, especially after the meeting started. This young girl began to tell us that she was addicted to two major drugs. When I say drugs, I'm not talking about weed and beer; I am talking about major, addictive stuff. The next thing she shared with me was that she was pregnant. Because I only spoke with her a few different times before that, I needed reminding of how old she was. Her response: "I am only fourteen." At this point, tears were flowing in every direction, from all three of us. Thankfully my female helper was there to hold that young lady and to communicate love to her in a much needed way.

Now, none of her predicaments are all that abnormal in this society. Isn't that a shame? This stuff is actually more common than we think. What broke my heart were two things. The first was the fact that she was fourteen. I cannot imagine how fearful this was for her, and worse, how potentially devastating it was for that child. The other thing that pained me was her reasoning for why she was doing drugs and having sex. This broken young lady explained to me that she had no real male influence in her life. She claimed that there were boys in her life that showed her affection, and though she hated what they made her do, at least she felt that someone wanted to be connected to her. Again, this is another textbook case of relational stupidity. This poor heart was broken long before these boys made her do anything. So, why wouldn't she go along with whatever they made her do?

A few years back, then-candidate Obama was campaigning for president for the first time. There was a specific question that was asked of him in regards to his stance on abortion. I remember that debate, and I remember chuckling at his response, because I wanted a specific answer to the question myself. Basically, he said that the answer to this was above his pay-grade. Until that moment in my office with this young lady, I had no grace for that old statement. That was until I said to myself, "This is just above my pay-grade." The question arose in my mind, *what am I going to say to bring hope to this young lady? I don't even know where to begin to bring her any sort of real and practical help.*

Suddenly, once I stopped scrambling to find the answer by myself, the Holy Spirit spoke to me and told me the answer. He said, "It is ME. The answer is in my activity, my gifts, my baptism, my voice, and my daily function within this heart, within this life, and within this soul." It suddenly made sense. It won't be by any wise or persuasive words but rather by a complete life makeover demonstrated by the Holy Spirit's power (see 1 Cor. 2:4).

Naturally, we want to tell this young lady to stay far away from these boys; we want to give her the best advice on how to handle the baby. Our initial thoughts are to go yell at Mom and immediately call Child Protective Services. We want to hold her, protect her; we want to detoxify her and stitch up her heart all on our own. It is like we are going to go shopping for her. We are picking out her new life, new gear, new body, and new mind. Now, none of this is wrong at all. In fact, in most cases, these steps must be taken. However, if you have ever tried to walk someone through a life change, you know that if they don't really want it, it is a big waste of time. Some people want change, but they aren't willing to do the difficult things to actually make it happen. Others are so lost that they don't even know where to begin or what to do. My conclusion is that without a complete Holy Spirit makeover, the proper metamorphosis won't ever take place.

Welcome to the all-important Holy Spirit chapter. There is no better way to end this book than by helping you begin your new life outside of the hotel. The Holy Spirit is your greatest fashion consultant for your new life, and your unlimited budget for a complete makeover. More than anything, he is the effervescent confidence you will need to thrive in this post-hotel world.

New Gear

After high school, I went through a difficult time. After all, life transitions can be a tempting time to book ourselves at the Heartbreak Hotel. For me, I gained a lot of weight. In fact, I gained nearly thirty pounds. For nearly three years, I was above *my* high school weight, and it made me insecure. Because of this, I resorted to huge shirts and baggy jeans, and I *hated* going shopping. February 2007 rolled around. My life was coming to a crossroads. My relationships were inconsistent, I didn't have any direction, and I was honestly just unhappy. I decided to do the only thing I thought was left to do: I was going to go on a fast. So, the day after the Super Bowl, I went on a liquid fast for the rest of the month. No solid food for twenty-two days. My hunger for direction so outweighed my hunger for food—or anything else, for that matter. It was during that time that the Holy Spirit directed me to Texas, and I also lost thirty pounds. More importantly, it was during that time that my confidence and countenance completely changed.

Because the Holy Spirit had all the room during that time, he was able to do all he could do in me. He dressed me with the confidence that I had been missing for years. For the first time, I really began to preach, and the doors of my life swung wide open. Immediately after the fast, I knew where I was going and how I was going to do it.

An encounter with the Spirit of God changes absolutely everything, literally everything. While in the Spirit, the powerless move mountains and the murderers exude compassion and love. Take Paul, for example—formerly Saul. He was known for torturing and killing Christians, but then he met the Spirit of God.

Meanwhile, Saul was uttering threats with every breath and was eager to kill the Lord's followers. So he went to the high priest. He requested letters addressed to the synagogues in Damascus, asking for their cooperation in the arrest of any followers of the Way he found there. He wanted to bring them—both men and women—back to Jerusalem in chains. As he was approaching Damascus on this mission, a light from heaven suddenly shone down around him. He fell to the ground and heard a voice saying to him, "Saul! Saul! Why are you persecuting me?" "Who are you, lord?" Saul asked. And the voice replied, "I am Jesus, the one you are persecuting! Now get up and go into the city, and you will be told what you must do." The men with Saul stood speechless, for they heard the sound of someone's voice but saw no one! Saul picked himself up off the ground, but when he opened his eyes he was blind. So his companions led him by the hand to Damascus. He remained there blind for three days and did not eat or drink (Acts 9:1–9).

As this man encounters Jesus, the Holy Spirit of God in Christ is halting the malice in Saul and putting a brand-new set of clothes on him. *The brilliance of the Spirit is that he blinds Saul so that he doesn't see it his old way anymore. When he opens his eyes from this encounter, he is never the same.* In fact, according to Scripture, the Lord even changes his name to Paul. It is a total redirection, a total shopping spree! Saul goes from being murderous to being Paul, who writes most of the New Testament of the Bible. As you can see, it is all in what you wear.

If you are in need of new gear, get on your face and encounter the Spirit of God. Ask him to put new clothes on you, instill confidence in you, and change who you once were for who you can be. Let him completely redefine your identity, once and for all!

An Extreme Makeover

So, not only did God re-invent Paul's identity, but he also directed his mission. When Paul opened his eyes, he saw the world completely different. *This moment in the presence of God didn't just change Paul, it changed the entire world.* Paul's encounter with Jesus empowered him to establish the handbook for the church today. His apostolic ministry is the standard for Christian living. We follow Paul as he follows Christ (see 1 Cor. 11:1). *The extreme makeover for our lives will be defined by the activity of power displayed in our everyday relationships, ministries, and purposes.* This power is available for the believer!

> But you will receive power when the Holy Spirit comes upon you. And you will be my witnesses, telling people about me everywhere— in Jerusalem, throughout Judea, in Samaria, and to the ends of the earth (Acts 1:8).

The function of the Holy Spirit is to bring forth vision for our lives in a way that we might have never known before. Just like Paul was formerly blind to the endless possibilities of the Spirit, we can easily miss out on the incredible journey of living with power. Who could we be? Where could we go? How can we go and change the world? Living outside of this hotel greatly increases our chance for greatness. Living in the Spirit greatly increases our chances of never slipping back in to the hotel.

Overflow

As I mentioned before, the Holy Spirit provides us unlimited resources. There is no limit of funds for this shopping spree of ours. As I close this chapter and this book, there is no other way to go out than to take complete advantage of this incredible giver of gifts.

Now, dear brothers and sisters, regarding your question about the special abilities the Spirit gives us. I don't want you to misunderstand this. You know that when you were still pagans, you were led astray and swept along in worshiping speechless idols. So I want you to know that no one speaking by the Spirit of God will curse Jesus, and no one can say Jesus is Lord, except by the Holy Spirit. There are different kinds of spiritual gifts, but the same Spirit is the source of them all. There are different kinds of service, but we serve the same Lord. God works in different ways, but it is the same God who does the work in all of us. A spiritual gift is given to each of us so we can help each other. To one person the Spirit gives the ability to give wise advice; to another the same Spirit gives a message of special knowledge. The same Spirit gives great faith to another, and to someone else the one Spirit gives the gift of healing. He gives one person the power to perform miracles, and another the ability to prophesy. He gives someone else the ability to discern whether a message is from the Spirit of God or from another spirit. Still another person is given the ability to speak in unknown languages, while another is given the ability to interpret what is being said. It is the one and only Spirit who distributes all these gifts. He alone decides which gift each person should have (1 Cor. 12:1–11).

There is an absolute overflow of gifts and opportunities while living life in the Spirit. Life outside this hotel is for *all*, but only some choose it (see John 3:16). The reason is because only some are willing to dive in completely. My youth pastor always made reference to his daughter at the pool. As she would lie on her water float to soak in the sun, her brothers would splash around in the water. Her girlish complaint was that they were getting her hair wet. His point is simply this: if she floats in the water, she should be willing to go all the way in too. If you are going to be out of this hotel, you might as well be all the way out. Indulge yourself fully in the Spirit. Let him get your hair wet, let him completely dunk you and pour all of these gifts and opportunities over your life. Don't just sit on the float. Jump all the way in!

If this is something that deeply interests you and you desire more of what these gifts offer, have a conversation with a pastor, leader, or someone who understands the Bible. Have an individual that you trust lay hands on your shoulders and pray for the full possibility of all God has for you.

Not Goodbye, See You Later

So, here we stand, finally outside the hotel! Not only do we have new clothes on, but also our bill has been paid in full. You know what else feels good? No luggage to drag around! I'll be honest though; there will be moments when you feel tempted to go back to the comfort of the old hotel. Before you make that mistake, remember this: *there is nothing to go back to*. You are completely free. You are a new creation. The old is dead and gone, and you are now ready to thrive in any circumstance. I am humbled you joined me on this journey and am fascinated that God has crossed our paths. I love you and am proud of you. This is only goodbye to the hotel, but we will meet again. Go!

Q 3s

1) Have you ever had an encounter with the Holy Spirit?

2) Do you feel that God is calling you to anything specific? (Ex. Ministry, Bible College, or go to another country for missions.)

3) Of the nine gifts mentioned in mentioned in 1 Corinthians 12:1–11, are there any you have experienced yourself?

P.S.

The completion of this book is a dream come true for me, but the completion of the work God has started in you is the only reason I wrote it. My prayer and my dream are for complete spiritual reformation and revival to come to our nation. It is without shame I declare my calling to America, to help usher in a new era of freedom. I love the world and the souls of the world, as they are God's heartbeat. I invest in the missionaries and ministries in Europe so that one day I might reap a great harvest in the United States. I close this book in a prayer for you and for our broken world ...

Pray With Me

Holy Spirit, impart hope and power to every mind and every life that has read or is reading this book. Speak to every broken heart, desperate soul, and visionless individual. Touch the world, from every corner, village, hut, and skyline. Destroy the walls of this hotel forever and break down the cultural, religious, racial, and political barriers that keep us from changing the world with the only hope, the only Gospel of peace. Jesus, shine your face on us and take not your Holy Spirit, ever. We ask for more vision, more power, more purpose, and more of the supernatural cross, forever. Amen.

CHAPTER 1

Glidewell, Jan. "Quotations About Living in the Present." Posted September 5, 2011. *The Quote Garden.* www.quotegarden.com/live-now.html. (Accessed November 18, 2011.)

CHAPTER 2

Miyazawa, Kenji. "Kenji Miyazawa Quotes." *Finest Quotes.* http://www.finestquotes.com. (Accessed November 18, 2011.)
Lombardi, Vince. "Great Vince Lombardi Quotes." Posted March 3, 2011. *Ten Great Vince Lombardi Quotes. www.enlightenyourday.com.* (Accessed November 18, 2011.)

CHAPTER 3

Francis, Brendan. "Quotations About Living in the Present." Posted September 5, 2011. *The Quote Garden.* www.quotegarden.com/live-now.html. (Accessed November 18, 2011.)

CHAPTER 4

St. Peter, Anthony. *The Greatest Quotations of All-Time.* Xlibris, 2010.
Moroder, Giorgio, and Tom Whitlock. "Danger Zone." *Top Gun.* Kenny Loggins. Sony, 1986. CD.
Groeschel, Craig. *Weird: Because Normal Isn't Working.* Grand Rapids, Mich.: Zondervan, 2011.

CHAPTER 5

Keller, Helen, and Roger Shattuck. *The World I Live In.* New York: The Century Co, 1908.

CHAPTER 6

Young, Wm. Paul. *The Shack*. Newbury Park, CA: Windblown Media, 2007.

CHAPTER 7

"Quotations About Heartache." Posted November 15, 2010. *The Quote Garden. www. quotegarden.com/heartache.html.* (Accessed November 18, 2011.)
Stanley, Andy. *Choosing to Cheat: Who Wins When Family and Work Collide?* Colorado Springs: Multnomah, 2003.

CHAPTER 8

Lewis, C. S. *The Problem of Pain*. New York: HarperCollins, 2001.

CHAPTER 9

Manning, Brennan. *The Signature of Jesus*. Colorado Springs: Multnomah Books, 1992.
Lewis, C. S. *Mere Christianity*. New York: HarperCollins, 2001.

CHAPTER 10

Maxwell, John C. *Talent is Never Enough: Discover the Choices that Will Take You Beyond Your Talent*. Nashville: Thomas Nelson, 2011.

CPSIA information can be obtained at www.ICGtesting.com
Printed in the USA
LVOW041359130312

272865LV00001B/1/P